ARTIFICIAL INTELLIGENCE
THE BASICS

Artificial Intelligence: The Basics is a concise and cutting-edge introduction to the fast-moving world of AI. The author Kevin Warwick, a pioneer in the field, examines issues of what it means to be man or machine and looks at advances in robotics that have blurred the boundaries. Topics covered include:

- how intelligence can be defined
- whether machines can 'think'
- sensory input in machine systems
- the nature of consciousness
- the controversial culturing of human neurons.

Exploring issues at the heart of the subject, this book is suitable for anyone interested in AI, and provides an illuminating and accessible introduction to this fascinating subject.

Kevin Warwick is Professor of Cybernetics at the University of Reading, UK, where he carries out research in artificial intelligence, control, robotics and biomedical engineering.

The Basics

ACTING
BELLA MERLIN

ANTHROPOLOGY
PETER METCALF

ARCHAEOLOGY (SECOND EDITION)
CLIVE GAMBLE

ART HISTORY
GRANT POOKE AND DIANA NEWALL

THE BIBLE
JOHN BARTON

BUDDHISM
CATHY CANTWELL

CRIMINAL LAW
JONATHAN HERRING

CRIMINOLOGY (SECOND EDITION)
SANDRA WALKLATE

ECONOMICS (SECOND EDITION)
TONY CLEAVER

EDUCATION
KAY WOOD

EVOLUTION
SHERRIE LYONS

EUROPEAN UNION (SECOND EDITION)
ALEX WARLEIGH-LACK

FILM STUDIES
AMY VILLAREJO

FINANCE (SECOND EDITION)
ERIK BANKS

HUMAN GENETICS
RICKI LEWIS

INTERNATIONAL RELATIONS
PETER SUTCH AND JUANITA ELIAS

ISLAM (SECOND EDITION)
COLIN TURNER

JUDAISM
JACOB NEUSNER

LANGUAGE (SECOND EDITION)
R.L. TRASK

LITERARY THEORY (SECOND EDITION)
HANS BERTENS

LOGIC
J.C. BEALL

MANAGEMENT
MORGEN WITZEL

MARKETING (SECOND EDITION)
KARL MOORE AND NIKETH PAREEK

PHILOSOPHY (FOURTH EDITION)
NIGEL WARBURTON

PHYSICAL GEOGRAPHY
JOSEPH HOLDEN

POETRY (SECOND EDITION)
JEFFREY WAINWRIGHT

POLITICS (FOURTH EDITION)
STEPHEN TANSEY AND NIGEL JACKSON

THE QUR'AN
MASSIMO CAMPANINI

RELIGION (SECOND EDITION)
MALORY NYE

RELIGION AND SCIENCE
PHILIP CLAYTON

RESEARCH METHODS
NICHOLAS WALLIMAN

ROMAN CATHOLICISM
MICHAEL WALSH

SEMIOTICS (SECOND EDITION)
DANIEL CHANDLER

SHAKESPEARE (SECOND EDITION)
SEAN MCEVOY

SOCIOLOGY
KEN PLUMMER

TELEVISION STUDIES
TOBY MILLER

TERRORISM
JAMES LUTZ AND BRENDA LUTZ

THEATRE STUDIES
ROBERT LEACH

WORLD HISTORY
PETER N. STEARNS

WORLD MUSIC
RICHARD NIDEL

ARTIFICIAL INTELLIGENCE

THE BASICS

Kevin Warwick

Routledge
Taylor & Francis Group

LONDON AND NEW YORK

First published 2012
by Routledge
2 Park Square, Milton Park, Abingdon, Oxon OX14 4RN

Simultaneously published in the USA and Canada
by Routledge
711 Third Avenue, New York, NY 10017 (8th Floor)

Routledge is an imprint of the Taylor & Francis Group, an informa business

British Library Cataloguing in Publication Data
A catalogue record for this book is available from the British Library

Library of Congress Cataloging in Publication Data
Warwick, K.
   Artificial intelligence: the basics/Kevin Warwick.
   p. cm. – (The basics)
   1. Artificial intelligence. 2. Intellect. I. Title.
   Q335.W365 2012
   006.3–dc22

                                                                2011013423

ISBN: 978-0-415-56482-3 (hbk)
ISBN: 978-0-415-56483-0 (pbk)
ISBN: 978-0-203-80287-8 (ebk)

Typeset in Bembo
by Wearset Ltd, Boldon, Tyne and Wear

CONTENTS

List of figures   vi
Preface   vii
Introduction   1

1   What is intelligence?   13
2   Classical AI   31
3   The philosophy of AI   60
4   Modern AI   88
5   Robots   116
6   Sensing the world   146

    Glossary   175
    Index   179

FIGURES

4.1	Basic schematic of a neuron	91
4.2	Basic model of a neuron	93
4.3	RAM neuron	99
5.1	Cyclops fish simulation	126
5.2	Cyclops fish evolved neural network	127
5.3	Seven dwarf robot	130
5.4	Simple robot maze	132

PREFACE

The field of Artificial Intelligence (AI) really came into existence with the birth of computers in and around the 1940s and 1950s. For the earlier period of its development, attention was clearly focused on getting computers to do things that, if a human did them, would be regarded as intelligent. Essentially, this involved trying to get computers to copy humans in some or all aspects of their behaviour. In the 1960s and 1970s this opened up a philosophical discussion as to just how close to a human brain a computer could be, and whether any differences that arose were really important. This period – referred to as 'classical AI' in this book – was, however, rather limited in its potential.

In the 1980s and 1990s we saw a whole new approach, a sort of bottom-up attack on the problem, effectively building artificial brains to bring about AI. This completely opened up the possibilities and created a whole new set of questions. No longer was AI restricted to merely copying human intelligence – now it could be intelligent in its own way. In some cases it could still be brought about by mimicking the way a human brain performed, but now it had the potential to be bigger, faster and better. The philosophical consequence of this was that now an artificial brain could potentially outperform a human brain.

In more recent years the field has really taken off. Real-world applications of AI, particularly in the finance, manufacturing and military sectors, are performing in ways with which the human brain simply cannot compete. Artificial brains are now being given their own body, with which to perceive the world in their own way and to move around in it and modify it as they see fit. They are being given the ability to learn, adapt and carry out their wishes with regard to humans. This raises all sorts of issues for the future.

The aim of this book has been to realise a truly modern and up-to-date look at the field of AI in its entirety. Classical AI is certainly looked at, but only as part of the total area. Modern AI is also considered with equal balance. In particular, some of the very latest research into embodied AI and growing biological AI is also discussed.

The intention is to provide a readable basic guide to the field of AI today – to see where it has come from and where it may be going. The main aim is to provide an introduction for someone not at all familiar with the topic. However, it may well also be of interest to those already involved in science, technology and even computing, who perhaps need to catch up with recent developments.

I would like to thank many people for their help in putting this book together. In particular, my colleagues and research students at the University of Reading, especially Mark Gasson, Ben Hutt, Iain Goodhew, Jim Wyatt, Huma Shah and Carole Leppard, all of whom have contributed significantly to the work described. I also wish to extend my gratitude to Andy Humphries of Taylor & Francis, who has pushed me to get the book completed despite many other conflicting calls on my time. Finally, I wish to thank my wife, Irena, for her patience, and my kids, Maddi and James, for their criticism.

Kevin Warwick
Reading, January 2011

INTRODUCTION

SYNOPSIS

In this opening chapter a brief overview is given of what the book is about, its aims and potential readership. A glimpse is also given of how the subject area has developed over the years, including mention of the key movers, important issues and breakthroughs. Essentially, the chapter provides a gentle helping hand to guide new readers into the subject. This chapter is not a necessity for those already familiar with the subject of AI, but nevertheless it could stimulate some thoughts or provide useful nuggets of information.

INTRODUCTION

The book is written as an introductory course text in Artificial Intelligence (AI), to provide material for a first course for students specialising in areas such as computer science, engineering and cybernetics. However, it can act as a background or reference text for all interested students, particularly in other branches of science and technology. It may also be useful as an introductory text for A-level students and even members of the general public who wish to get an overview of the field in an easily digestible form.

The subject area has shifted dramatically in the last few years and the text is intended to give a modern view of the subject. Classical AI techniques are certainly covered, but in a limited way – the goal is an all-encompassing, modern text.

The content of the book covers aspects of AI involving philosophy, technology and basic methods. Although indicators are given of AI programming with basic outlines, the book does not attend to the details of writing actual programs and does not get bogged down with intricacies concerning the differences between programming languages. The main aim is to give an overview of AI – an essential guide that doesn't go too heavily into depth on any specific topic. Pointers are given as to further texts which can take the reader deeper into a particular area of interest.

Although the text provides a general overview, potentially accessible by the general public, it has been written with academic rigour. Some previous texts have been directed more towards a fun book for children – this book is not of that type.

EARLY HISTORY OF AI

There are strong links between the development of computers and the emergence of AI. However, the seeds of AI were sown long before the development of modern computers. Philosophers such as Descartes considered animals in terms of their machine perform-ance, and automatons were the precursors of the humanoid robots of today. But artificial beings can be traced back even further, to stories of the Prague Golem, or even further to Greek myths such as Pygmalion's Galatea.

The strongest immediate roots probably date back to the work of McCulloch and Pitts, who, in 1943, described mathematical models (called perceptrons) of neurons in the brain (brain cells) based on a detailed analysis of the biological originals. They not only indicated how neurons either fire or do not fire (are 'on' or 'off'), thereby operating in a switching binary fashion, but also showed how such neurons could learn and hence change their action with respect to time.

Perhaps one of the greatest pioneers of the field was a British scientist, Alan Turing. In the 1950s (long before the computers of today appeared), Turing wrote a seminal paper in which he attempted to answer the question 'Can a machine think?' To even ask the question was, at the time, revolutionary, but to also come up with an applicable test (commonly known as the Turing Test) with which to answer the question was provocative in the extreme. The test is considered in detail in Chapter 3.

It was shortly after this that Marvin Minsky and Dean Edmonds built what could be described as the first AI computer, based on a network of the neuron models of McCulloch and Pitts. At the same time, Claude Shannon considered the possibility of a computer playing chess and the type of strategies needed in order to decide which move to make next. In 1956, at the instigation of John McCarthy, along with Minsky and Shannon, researchers came together at Dartmouth College in the USA for the first workshop celebrating the new field of AI. It was here that many of the subsequent classical foundations of the subject were first laid.

THE MIDDLE AGES OF AI DEVELOPMENT

In the 1960s the most profound contribution to the field was arguably the General Problem Solver of Newell and Simon. This was a multi-purpose program aimed at simulating, using a computer, some human problem-solving methods. Unfortunately the technique employed was not particularly efficient, and because of the time taken and memory requirements to solve even relatively straightforward real problems, the project was abandoned.

The other significant contribution of the 1960s was that of Lotfi Zadeh, with his introduction of the idea of 'fuzzy' sets and systems – meaning that computers do not have to operate in a merely binary, logical format, but can also perform in a human-like, 'fuzzy' way. This technique and its spin-offs are considered in Chapter 4.

Other than these examples, the 1960s was perhaps a time of some foolhardy claims regarding the potential of AI to copy and even perhaps recreate the entire workings of the human brain within a very short space of time. An observation in hindsight is that trying to get a computer to operate in exactly the same way as a human brain was rather like trying to make an aeroplane fly in the same way as a bird. In the latter case one would miss out on the good characteristics of the aeroplane, and so it was that AI research at this time missed out on much of the good points on offer from computers.

Unfortunately (and quite surprisingly), some of the limited thinking from the 1960s persists today. Some present textbooks (some even under the guise of modern AI) still concentrate merely on the classical approach of trying to get a computer to copy human intelligence, without truly considering the extent and exciting possibilities of different types of AI — in terms of machines being intelligent in their own way, not merely copying human intelligence.

In this period, considerable effort did go into making computers understand and converse in natural, human language, rather than their more direct machine code. This was partly driven by Turing's ideas of intelligence, but also partly by a desire for computers to more readily interface with the real world.

One of the best English-speaking computer programs was Joseph Weisenbaum's ELIZA. Indeed, this was the first of what have become known as 'Chatterbots'. Even at this relatively early stage, some of its conversations were sufficiently realistic that some users occasionally were fooled into thinking they were communicating with a human rather than a computer.

In fact, ELIZA generally gave a canned response or simply repeated what had been said to it, merely rephrasing the response with a few basic rules of grammar. However, it was shown that such an action appeared to adequately copy, to some extent, some of the conversational activities of humans.

THE DARK AGES OF AI RESEARCH

After the excitement of the 1960s, with substantial research funding and claims of what would shortly be achieved in terms of AI replicating human intelligence, the 1970s proved to be something of a let down, and in many ways was a Dark Age for AI. Some of the more optimistic claims of the 1960s raised expectations to an extremely high level, and when the promised results failed to be realised, much of the research funding for AI disappeared.

At the same time the field of neural networks — computers copying the neural make-up of the brain — came to a halt almost overnight due to a scathing attack from Marvin Minsky and Seymour Papert on the inability of perceptrons to generalise in order to deal with certain types of relatively simple problems — something we will look at in Chapter 4.

It must be realised, however, that in the 1970s the capabilities of computers and therefore AI programs were quite limited in comparison with those of today. Even the best of the programs could only deal with simple versions of the problems they were aimed at solving; indeed, all the programs at that time were, in some sense, 'toy' programs.

Researchers had in fact run into several fundamental limits that would not be overcome until much later. The main one of these was limited computing power. There was nowhere near enough speed or memory for really useful tasks – an example of this from the time was Ross Quillan's natural language machine, which had to get by with a total vocabulary of 20 words!

However, the main problem was that AI tasks, such as getting a computer to communicate in a natural language or to understand the content of a picture in anything like a human way, required a lot of information and a lot of processing power, even to operate at a very low, restricted level. General, everyday objects in an image can be difficult for computers to discern, and what humans regard as common-sense reasoning about words and objects actually requires a lot of background information.

If the technical difficulties faced in the 1970s were not enough, the field also became an acceptable topic of interest to philosophers. For example, John Searle came up with his Chinese room argument (which we look at in Chapter 3) to show that a computer cannot be said to 'understand' the symbols with which it communicates. Further, he argued, because of this the machine cannot necessarily be described as 'thinking' – as Turing had previously postulated – purely in terms of symbol manipulation.

Although many practical researchers simply got on with their jobs and avoided the flak, several philosophers (such as Searle) gave the strong impression that the actual achievements of AI would always be severely limited. Minsky said, of these people: 'They misunderstand, and should be ignored.' As a result, a lot of in-fighting occurred, which took the focus away from technical developments, and towards philosophical arguments which (in hindsight) many now see to be red herrings.

Almost standing alone at the time, John McCarthy considered that how the human brain operates and what humans do is not directly relevant for AI. He felt that what were really needed were machines that could solve problems – not necessarily computers that think in exactly the same way people do. Minsky was critical of this, claiming that understanding objects and conversing, to be done well, required a computer to think like a person. And so the arguments went on...

THE AI RENAISSANCE

The 1980s saw something of a revival in AI. This was due to three factors.

First, many researchers followed McCarthy's lead and continued to develop AI systems from a practical point of view. To put it simply, they just got on with it. This period saw the development of 'expert systems', which were designed to deal with a very specific domain of knowledge – hence somewhat avoiding the arguments based on a lack of 'common sense'. Although initially piloted in the 1970s, it was in the 1980s that such systems began to be used for actual, practical applications in industry.

Second, although the philosophical discussions (and arguments) continued, particularly as regards to whether or not a machine could possibly think in the same way as a human, they seemed to do so largely independently of the practical AI work that was occurring. The two schools simply proceeded with their own thing, the AI developers realising practical industrial solutions without necessarily claiming that computers should or could behave like humans.

Third, the parallel development of robotics started to have a considerable influence on AI. In this respect a new paradigm arose in the belief that to exhibit 'real' intelligence, a computer needs to have a body in order to perceive, move and survive in the world. Without such skills, the argument goes, how can a computer ever be expected to behave in the same way as a human? Without these abilities, how could a computer experience common sense? So, the advent of a cybernetic influence on AI put much more emphasis on building AI from the bottom up, the sort of approach, in fact, originally postulated by McCulloch and Pitts.

TO THE PRESENT

Gradually, the emergent field of AI found its feet. Industrial applications of AI grew in number and it started to be used in expansive areas, such as financial systems and the military. In these areas it was shown to be not only a replacement for a human operative, but also, in many cases, able to perform much better. Applications of AI in these areas have now expanded enormously, to the extent that financial companies that used to earn their money from advising clients now make much bigger profits from developing AI systems to sell to and service for their clients.

The period since the start of the 1990s has also seen various milestones reached and targets hit. For example, on 11 May 1997, Deep Blue became the first chess-playing computer system to beat a reigning, world chess champion (Garry Kasparov) at his own game. In another vein, on 14 March 2002 Kevin Warwick (the author) was the first to successfully link the human nervous system directly with a computer to realise a new combined form of AI – but more of that in a moment. On 8 October 2005 it was announced that a Stanford University robot had won the DARPA Grand Challenge by driving autonomously for 131 miles along an unrehearsed desert trail. Meanwhile, in 2009, the Blue Brain Project team announced that they had successfully simulated parts of a rat's cortex.

For the most part, such successes as these were not, in any case, due to a newly invented form of technology, but rather to pushing the limits with the technology available. In fact, Deep Blue, as a computer, was over ten million times faster than the Ferranti computer system taught to play chess in 1951. The ongoing, year-on-year, dramatic increase in computing power is both followed and predicted by what has become known as Moore's Law.

Moore's Law indicates that the speed and memory capacity of computers doubles every two years. It means that the earlier problems faced by AI systems are quite rapidly being overcome by sheer computing power. Interestingly, each year sees some claim or other in a newspaper that Moore's Law will come to an end due to a limiting factor such as size, heat, cost, etc. However, each year new technological advances mean that available computing power doubles and Moore's Law just keeps on going.

On top of this, the period has also seen novel approaches to AI emerge. One example is the method of 'intelligent agents'. This is a modular approach, which could be said to be mimicking the brain in some ways – bringing together different specialist agents to tackle each problem, in the same sort of way that a brain has different regions for use in different situations. This approach also fits snugly with computer science methods in which different programs are associated with different objects or modules – the appropriate objects being brought together as required.

An intelligent agent is much more than merely a program. It is a system in itself in that it must perceive its environment and take actions to maximise its chances of success. That said, it is true that in their simplest form, intelligent agents are merely programs that solve specific problems. However, such agents can be individual robot or machine systems, operating physically autonomously.

As is described in Chapter 4, as well as agents, lots of other new approaches have arisen in the field of AI during this period. Some of these have been decidedly more mathematical in nature, such as probability and decision theory. Meanwhile, neural networks and concepts from evolution, such as genetic algorithms, have played a much more influential role.

It is certainly the case that particular actions can be construed as being intelligent acts (in humans or animals) up to the point that they can be performed (often more effectively) by a computer. It is also the case that a lot of new developments in AI have found their way into more general applications. In doing so, they often lose the tag of 'AI'. Good examples of this can be found with data mining, speech recognition and much of the decision making presently carried out in the banking sector. In each case, what was originally AI has become regarded as just another part of a computer program.

THE ADVENT OF WIRELESS

One of the key technologies that became a practical reality in the 1990s was wireless technology as a form of communication for computers, following on from widespread introduction and use of the internet. From an AI perspective, this completely changed the playing field. Until that time what existed were standalone computers, the power and capabilities of which could be directly compared with standalone human brains – the normal set up. With networked computers becoming commonplace, rather than considering each computer separately, it became realistically necessary to consider the entire network as one, large intelligent brain with much distribution – called distributed intelligence.

Thanks to wireless technology, connectivity is an enormous advantage for AI over human intelligence – in its present-day standalone form. At first it was mainly a means whereby computers could communicate rapidly with each other. However, it has quickly become the case that large pockets of memory are dispersed around a network, specialism is spread and information flows freely and rapidly. It has changed the human outlook on security and privacy and has altered the main means by which humans communicate with each other.

HAL 9000

In 1968 Arthur C. Clarke wrote *2001: A Space Odyssey*, which was later turned into a film of the same name by Stanley Kubrick. The story contains a character, HAL 9000. HAL is a machine whose intelligence is either the same as or better than human intelligence. Indeed it/he exhibits human traits of meaningful emotions and philosophy. Although HAL was merely a fictional machine, it nevertheless became something of a milestone to be reached in the field of AI. In the late 1960s many believed that such a form of AI would exist by 2001 – particularly as HAL was based on underpinning science of the time.

Various people have asked why we didn't have some form of HAL, or at least a close approximation, by 2001. Minsky grumbled that too much time had been spent on industrial computing rather than on a fundamental understanding of issues such as common sense. In a similar vein, others complained that AI research concentrated on simple neuron models, such as the perceptron, rather than on an attempt to get a much closer model of original human brain cells.

Perhaps the answer as to why we didn't have HAL by 2001 is an amalgamation of these issues, and more. We simply didn't have the focused drive to achieve such a form of AI. No one put up the money to do it and no research team worked on the project. In many ways – such as networking, memory and speed – we had already realised something much more powerful than HAL by 2001, but emotional, moody reflections within a computer did not (and probably still do not) have a distinctive role to play, other than perhaps in feature films.

For the guru Ray Kurzweil, the reason for the non-appearance of HAL is merely computer power and, using Moore's Law, his prediction is that machines with human-level intelligence will appear by 2029. Of course, what is meant by 'human-level intelligence' is a big question. My own prediction in my earlier book, *March of the Machines*, was not too far away from Kurzweil though – machines will have an intelligence that is too much for humans to handle by 2050.

TO THE FUTURE

Much of the classical philosophy of AI (as discussed in Chapter 3) is based largely on the concept of a brain or computer as a sort of standalone entity – a disembodied brain in a jar, so to speak. In the real world, however, humans interact with the world around them through sensors and motor skills.

What is of considerable interest now, and will be even more so in the future, is the effect of the body on the intellectual abilities of that body's brain. Ongoing research aims at realising an AI system in a body – **embodiment** – so it can experience the world, whether it be the real version of the world or a virtual or even simulated world. Although the study of AI is still focused on the AI brain in question, the fact that it does have a body with which it can interact with the world is seen as important.

As we step into the future, perhaps the most exciting area of AI research is that in which AI brains are grown from biological neural tissue – typically obtained from either a rat or a human. Particular details of the procedures involved and the methods required to launder and successfully grow living biological neural tissue are given in Chapter 5. In this case, the AI is no longer based on a computer system as we know it, but rather on a biological brain that has been grown afresh.

This topic is certainly of interest in its own right as a new form of AI, and is potentially useful in the future for household robots. However, it also provides a significant new area of study in terms of its questioning of many of the philosophical assumptions from classical AI. Essentially, such philosophy discussed the difference between human intelligence and that of a silicon machine. In this novel research area, however, AI brains can be grown from human neurons, by building them up into something like an AI version of a human brain type, thus blurring what was a crisp divide between two distinctly different brain styles.

CYBORGS

It could be said that when a biological AI brain is given a technological robot body then it is a type of cyborg – a *cyb*ernetic *org*anism (part animal/human, part technology/machine) – with an embodied brain. This area of research is the most exciting of all – the direct link between an animal and a machine for the betterment (in terms of performance) of both. Such a cyborg as discussed is just one potential version. Indeed, neither the normal researched form of cyborg nor that usually encountered in science fiction is of this type.

The type of cyborg more regularly encountered is in the form of a human who has, implanted in them, integral technology which is linked to a computer which thereby gives them abilities above those of the human norm – meaning a cyborg has skills that a human does not. These skills can be physical and/or mental and can pertain to intelligence. In particular, we will see that an AI brain is usually (excluding a biological AI brain) very different from a human brain, and these differences can be realised in terms of advantages (particularly for AI).

Reasons for the creation of cyborgs generally revolve around enhancing the performance of the human brain by linking it directly with a machine brain. The combined brain can then, potentially at least, function with characteristic features from both its constituent parts – a cyborg could therefore possibly have better memory, faster math skills, better senses, multidimensional thought and improved communication skills when compared with a human brain. To date, experiments have successfully shown both sensory enhancement and a new form of communication for cyborgs. Although not specifically dealt with in this text, it is felt that the material covered in Chapters 5 and 6 will put the reader in good stead for a follow-on study in this field.

CONCLUDING REMARKS

This chapter has set the scene for the rest of the book, giving a brief overview of AI's historical development and some of the key developments. In doing so, some of the movers and shakers in the field have been introduced.

In the following text, after a gentle introduction (Chapter 1) to the overall concept of intelligence, Chapters 2 and 3 concentrate on the classical AI methods that were originally introduced. Chapters 4 and 5 then consider ongoing, modern and more futuristic approaches. You will find that the more novel, up-to-date sections of Chapters 4 and 5 are probably not encountered in most other AI textbooks – even when such books are called *Artificial Intelligence* or *AI: A Modern Approach*. Chapter 6 then considers how an AI can perceive the world through its sensor system.

Enjoy!

KEY TERM

embodiment

FURTHER READING

1   *AI: A Guide to Intelligent Systems* by M. Negnevitsky, published by Addison Wesley, 1st edition, 2001. This is quite a general book which keeps mathematics to a minimum and provides a reasonably broad coverage of classical AI with little jargon. It is a good introductory guide, based on lectures given by the author. Unfortunately, it doesn't deal with topics such as robotics, biological AI or sensing.

2   *Artificial Intelligence: A Beginner's Guide* by B. Whitby, published by OneWorld, 2008. This is quite a reasonable, level-headed overview text. It is more concerned with ethical issues and is fairly conservative, but well posed. It doesn't explain topics in any depth, however.

3   *Understanding Artificial Intelligence*, edited by *Scientific American* staff, Warner Books, 2002. This is actually a collection of essays on the subject. Although mostly concerned with the philosophy of AI, it gives a feel for what different experts consider to be the main issues.

1

WHAT IS INTELLIGENCE?

SYNOPSIS

Before embarking on a tour of an artificial form of intelligence, here we take a look at what intelligence actually is in humans, animals and machines. The important aspects of mental make-up are considered, some myths chopped down to size and comparisons are made between intelligence in the different entities. For example, what is the intelligence of a spider? What does it mean for a machine to be intelligent? How would human intelligence be regarded by an alien? Clearly the subjective nature of intelligence is important.

DEFINING INTELLIGENCE: AN IMPOSSIBLE TASK?

It is important, before looking into 'artificial' intelligence, to try to understand what exactly intelligence is in the first place. What do we mean when we say a person, animal or thing is intelligent? In fact, everyone has a different concept based on their own experiences and views, dependent on what they think is important and what is not. This can easily change – what may be deemed to be intelligent at one time and place may not be so deemed later or elsewhere.

As an example, in the *New English Dictionary* of 1932, intelligence was defined as: 'The exercise of understanding: intellectual power: acquired knowledge: quickness of intellect.' Clearly, at that time an emphasis was placed on knowledge and mental speed, with a leaning towards human intelligence. More recently, the *Macmillan*

Encyclopedia of 1995 stated that 'Intelligence is the ability to reason and to profit by experience. An individual's level of intelligence is determined by a complex interaction between their heredity and environment.'

In the 1900s, Binet (the inventor of the IQ test) picked on judgement, common sense, initiative and adaptability as 'essential ingredients of intelligence'. Recently, intelligence has even been linked with spiritual awareness or emotions. Clearly, intelligence in humans is important but it is not the only example of intelligence and we must not let it override all else. If we are comparing intellectual ability between humans, then standard tests of one type or another are useful. However, we need here to consider intelligence in a much broader sense, particularly if we are to investigate intelligence in machines.

ANIMAL INTELLIGENCE

It is well worth considering intelligence in creatures other than humans in order to open our minds to different possibilities. Here, we will look at a few to consider aspects of intelligence such as communication, planning and some of the terms just defined, such as initiative, reasoning and quickness of intellect.

Bees exhibit individual behavioural characteristics within a tightly knit society. They appear to communicate with each other by means of a complex dance routine. When one bee returns from a pollen collection expedition, it performs a dance at the hive entrance, wiggling its bottom and moving forward in a straight line. The distance moved is proportional to the distance of the pollen source and the angle moved indicates the angle between the source and the sun. In this way, other bees can learn which is a good direction to fly.

There are over 30,000 different species of spider, each with its own speciality. Water spiders, for example, live in ponds and build an air-filled diving bell out of silk. They then wait underwater for passing prey such as shrimps. At the right moment the spider pounces to deliver a fatal bite, pulling the prey back into its lair before devouring it.

Many creatures have been witnessed exhibiting learning abilities. A good example of this is the octopus. By training one octopus to choose between objects of different colour, experiments have shown how a second octopus who has watched the first through a glass partition can then carry out the exact same decision-making process.

Many creatures use tools. An unusual example of this is the green heron. Herons have been seen dropping morsels of food into water where fish are expected to be. When the fish swims to take the bait, the heron catches it.

Because of their genetic links to humans, chimpanzees are the most widely studied non-human animal. They can: communicate (even with humans); plan hunting trips; use a variety of tools in sequenced order for food collection or climbing; play; put the blame on others; and even use devious ploys to gain sexual favours – this on top of exhibiting basic learning skills. But perhaps it is easier to measure such abilities when they are close to those of humans. The capabilities of creatures such as spiders, whales or slugs can be extremely difficult to give value to if they are meaningless to humans.

BRAIN SIZE AND PERFORMANCE

It could be argued that one way in which direct comparisons can be made is in terms of brain size, relative numbers of brain cells (neurons) and complexity. Comparing a human brain of approximately 100 billion neurons with a sea slug consisting of 8–9 neurons appears to make a good start. However, between species brain size, neuron size and connectivity all vary tremendously. Even between humans there can be large variations. In the past this was used to 'prove' all sorts of results.

In Germany in 1911 the minimum requirement for a professor was a head circumference of 52 centimetres. This was used to discriminate against women; Bayerthal, a leading medical physicist of the time stated: 'We do not have to ask for the head circumference of women of genius – they do not exist.' At the same time, Gustave Le Bon, a French scientist of note pointed out that, on average, women had brains which were closer in size to gorillas than they were to those of men!

These serve as good examples of trying to use some sort of measure to come to the conclusion that was wanted (in this case by some men) in the first place. This is something that must be avoided at all costs in studying intelligence, yet it is one that has appeared time and again in studies. That said, it is also inappropriate to overlook observable differences simply because they are deemed to be not politically correct.

One issue with brain size and a count of neurons is the definition of what exactly constitutes a brain. For an individual creature this might be answered quite simply in terms of the main group of central neural-type cells (in a creature's head). In humans, approximately 99% of neurons are in the skull, with the other 1% in the nervous system. In many insects the divide is more like 50–50 due to their dependence on rapid processing of sensory input. In machines, however, the brain is often networked – leading to a conclusion that the effective brain size is the total number of neural-type cells in the network, rather than merely those in one central repository.

A pure count of brain cells is extremely problematic, even in humans. As an example, consider a person who has had a stroke such that their neuron count is significantly reduced due to neural death over a section of the brain. Yet they may still be able to perform in many ways much better than many 'normal' individuals.

Perhaps energy usage would be a better start point. Brains are highly expensive in this regard. Human brain metabolism accounts for as much as 22% of total body requirements. In a chimpanzee this figure drops to 9%, and in insects is lower still. In machines that do not move, apart from cooling fans and indicating lights, not far short of 100% of its energy requirements are used for information processing.

SENSING AND MOVEMENT

Intelligence is an important part of an individual's make-up. However, this depends not on their brain alone, but also on how it senses and activates things in the world around it. How the world is perceived by that individual depends on the functioning of their brain, their senses and their actuators (e.g. muscles).

Humans have five senses: vision, hearing, taste, touch and smell. This gives us a limited range of inputs. We cannot sense many signal frequencies; for example, we do not have ultraviolet, ultrasonic or X-ray sensory input. Our perception of the world is therefore quite limited – there is a lot going on around us that we have no idea about because we cannot sense it.

At the same time, another creature or a machine with different senses could be witnessing a major event which a human would know nothing about. A being's senses need to be taken into account when considering intelligence. Just because a being is not the same as a human – for example, if it senses the world in a different way – this does not necessarily make it better or worse, merely different.

The success of a being depends on it performing well, or at least adequately, in its own environment. Intelligence plays a critical part in this success. Different creatures and machines succeed in their own way. We should not consider that humans are the only intelligent beings on Earth; rather, we need to have an open concept of intelligence to include a breadth of human and non-human possibilities.

The story is much the same in terms of movement. Humans are able to manipulate the world in various ways and to move around within it. Each being has different abilities in this respect, depending on what their life role is. It is not appropriate to say something is not (or less) intelligent because it cannot do some specific task. For example, it would be wrong to say that a creature or machine is stupid because it cannot make a cup of tea – this is a very human task. Only in comparing humans should such a task even be considered as some form of measure.

Based on this broadening discussion, a more general definition of intelligence might be: 'The variety of information-processing processes that collectively enable a being to autonomously pursue its survival.'

With this as a basis, not only can intelligence in animals and machines be respected and studied for what it is, but also intelligence in humans can be put into perspective in terms of merely serving as one example. Clearly, this definition is open to much criticism, but it is felt to be a substantial improvement on those given at the start of the chapter, which have far too strong a human bias to them. It could be argued that the earlier definitions are not explaining intelligence in general, but only human intelligence.

ALIEN VIEW

An interesting way to consider the problem of intelligence is to think of yourself as an alien from another planet, inspecting Earth from afar. What would you consider the intelligent life forms on Earth to be? Could they be vehicles, networks, water, clouds, animals, bacteria, televisions? Presumably you would apply some tests based on your own concepts of life form and intelligence. So, if you are living on a planet for which the main sensory input is a type of infrared signal, then your view of Earth may well not include humans as an intelligent life form.

Even considering what we as humans define as being the basics of life could lead to apparently strange conclusions. From basic biology we could consider the following as indications: nutrition, excretion, movement, growth, irritability, respiration, production (production rather than reproduction as humans produce, they do not 'reproduce' other than through cloning, which is ethically questionable).

From an alien standpoint, even a telephone exchange or communications network satisfies these qualities of life – perhaps much more obviously than humans do – merely in terms of electrical pulses rather than chemical. From an alien viewpoint it could be concluded (even now) that a complex global networked intelligence on Earth was being served by small drone-like simpler beings – humans.

SUBJECTIVE INTELLIGENCE

Intelligence is an extremely complex, multi-faceted entity. In each being it consists of many different aspects. Intelligence is also subjective in terms of the group by which it is being viewed and the group being viewed. For any particular group that is considering intelligence, what are and what are not regarded as intelligent acts are dependent on the views of that group and are steeped in the social and cultural trappings of its members.

When a puppy walks by the side of a person, this could be considered to be an intelligent thing to do or simply as the puppy satisfying a trivial programmed goal. When a human is able to rapidly calculate answers to mathematical questions or accurately remember a series of facts on a particular topic, these could be regarded as intelligent acts – indeed the person could be called a 'mastermind' – or they could be regarded as a mere entertainment exercise.

With differences between species the problem is exacerbated due to their different mental and physical capabilities and requirements. For humans studying different species (I include machines here) it is therefore important to try to recognise aspects of intelligence for what they are worth within that species rather than merely in terms of how they compare to aspects of human intelligence.

Between humans we need to try and retain a scientific basis for our analysis of intelligence rather than to pamper to social stereotypes. For example, why is it that knowledge about politics, classical music or fine art is seen by some to be more indicative of intelligence than knowledge about football, pop music or pornography? Why is it that playing music by Mozart to a baby while still in the womb is considered, by some, to make the baby more intelligent, whereas playing music by the Rolling Stones is considered to be dangerous? Is there any scientific basis at all for such conclusions? I think not. Where are the conclusive scientific studies that have shown these things to be so? There are none.

Unfortunately, we can quickly run into the problem previously mentioned, in that we already have a conclusion and we try to fit certain observations to match that conclusion and ignore others that do not match. If you wish to succeed at school or university, it is better (I take these merely as examples) to learn about fine art or classical music rather than football or pop music as these latter subjects can be seen as disruptive or a complete waste of time. From those who succeed in these areas of education will come the teachers and professors of the future who, in turn, because of the subjective nature of intelligence, will value those who toe the line and follow the lead of learning about fine art or classical music – those who perform well in the areas considered to be proper by the teachers themselves, who define the subject areas. And so it goes on.

A strong social bias runs through such human educational systems and this can result in completely different values associated with subject areas. An individual can be regarded by others as being stupid simply because they do not know particular facts, cannot carry out specific mathematical calculations or deal with some aspect of everyday life. Clearly, this is merely representative of one aspect of their intelligence – nothing more and nothing less.

Despite this, humans often tend to use the same approach to make comparisons with other creatures or machines. Sometimes we do not give value to non-human abilities, partly because we do not understand them. Conversely, we give value to animals copying some aspect of human abilities – for example, some consider dolphins to be intelligent simply because they do some tricks and are friendly to humans, whereas sharks are sometimes regarded as mindless killing machines because humans do not necessarily have the same mind set and values as a shark.

Each individual has their own concept of intelligence with which they can measure others, both human and non-human, in order to make comparisons – often to come to the conclusion that one individual is more or less intelligent than another. A group's view of intelligence arises from a consensus between individuals who hold similar social and cultural beliefs and share common assumptions. Everyone's concept also partly reflects their own personal qualities.

When assessing the intelligence of a non-human, possibly a machine, if we wish to put it down and claim in some way that it is not as good as a human, then we can certainly make comparisons of the non-human's abilities in a field in which humans perform well. We can, of course, compare human abilities with a non-human in a field in which the non-human performs well – however, the result would not be so good for humans, so we don't tend to do such a thing.

In assessing the intelligence of an individual we really need to get to grips with the physical make-up of that individual, their mental make-up, their social requirements (if any) and the environment in which they live and perform.

IQ TESTS

It is a basic feature of human nature to compare and compete. Indeed, our survival as a species on Earth depends on such basic qualities. In sport we wish to see which human can run fastest, lift the heaviest weights or eat the most eggs. We acknowledge that physically people tend to have their own specialities. Sometimes we look for broader physical abilities, such as in the decathlon, but generally it is performance in one particular competition that is the focus. Importantly, we do not try to come up with a single number (a quotient) which defines an individual's physical abilities – a PQ (physical quotient).

When it comes to intelligence it is apparent that people, once again, tend to have their own specialities. Perhaps someone is better at music, one aspect of math or maybe they are good at debating. These are very different talents. Yet for some reason we often appear to want to assign a level of intelligence to each human in terms of a simple numerical description – their IQ (intelligence quotient) – to the extent that this number (in one form or another) defines what they are allowed to do in society.

In the nineteenth century (and even before) there were many intelligence tests of one type or another. For example, Frances Galton exhibited a series of tests in the Science Museum in London. These included: putting in weight order a number of boxes each different by 1 g; distinguishing how close two points could be placed on the back of your hand before you couldn't tell the difference; and measuring the speed of response to a noise. However, there was deemed to be no firm scientific basis for such tests in that there were no repeatable statistical links between the results of the test and how well individuals performed in their schooling.

The IQ test itself was originally formulated by Alfred Binet in 1904. He was charged with developing a simple method by which children who would struggle in the normal school environment could be easily identified.

He concentrated on faculties such as memory, comprehension, imagination, moral understanding, motor skills and attention. The final version of his test, which was aimed at children 3–12 years old, was made up of 30 parts which children worked through in sequence from the start until they could no longer continue. The number reached was the 'mental age' of the child. By subtracting the answer from the child's actual age, so the child's intellectual level was revealed.

Binet's test was originally required in order to select the appropriate schooling for children, by predicting their likely performance from the result of a simple set of questions. It was never intended as an indicator of the child's general level of intelligence. In fact, Binet himself worried that children would be seen as unintelligent purely on the basis of a poor performance in the test. Despite this, subsequent versions of Binet's test were used around the world for people of all ages to decide on the type of schooling they should receive, whether they should be allowed entry to a country (the USA) and even whether they should be sterilised (Virginia up to 1972).

The use of such tests and their validity has been severely questioned in recent times. In fact, validity tends to have been shown in terms of statistical links insofar as those who do well in school exams tend to also do well in IQ tests. Whether this means IQ tests actually indicate anything at all about intelligence remains an unanswered question. However, there are strong statistical correlations between exam performance (and hence IQ test performance) and job status (interestingly, not so with job performance).

IQ test performance gives a likely indication of general exam performance and hence such tests have been used extensively to show the effects of lifestyle and activity – whatever one thinks of IQ tests such results are fascinating.

Changing one's IQ score by more than three points is quite a strong indicator. Consider, then, that regular vitamin C intake in children has been shown to improve their IQ score by eight points (on average). Meanwhile, pollution appears to have little effect – doubling lead intake (pretty heavy) reduces one's score by only one point. In later life, bottle-fed babies fare worse on IQ tests than breast-fed babies and children who regularly use a dummy score 3–5 points lower (in later life) than those who do not. Children whose mothers were 35 or older score six points higher, and so it goes on. Obviously there are social links associated with each of the indicators mentioned and it is difficult, if not impossible, to separate items from such aspects.

Years ago (mostly for fun) I was involved in a study to look at the effects of what a person does immediately before taking an IQ test to see how it affected results, on the basis that if it affected results of IQ tests then it would probably be the same for exams. So we enlisted 200 first-year students to take one IQ test then carry out a different activity with specific nutrition. After half an hour they took a second IQ test. We compared the results to see which results had improved and which had declined. We were not bothered about the actual results obtained, but rather whether they had improved or declined and how this related to the activity and nutrition.

We found that those who drank coffee increased their score by three points, whereas those that ate chocolate decreased their score by three points. The scores of those who watched a chat show on TV increased by five points, whereas those who read (as in swotting) lowered their score by six points and those who played with a construction toy lowered their score by four points.

Although the media portrayed this in the form that watching TV chat shows makes you more intelligent, what it actually showed was that if you want to improve your exam performance, in the half hour before the exam it might be best to chill out, have a cup of coffee and watch TV, particularly a programme you don't have to think about too much. It certainly doesn't appear to be good to use your brain (by swotting) immediately prior to taking an exam.

While IQ tests can be fun, their links with intelligence appear to be solely based on correlations with exam performance. Like exams, they are extremely subjective in that an individual needs to know details in a specific area in order to perform well in a particular exam. This is also borne out in IQ tests. The tests we carried out involved spatial awareness, number sequences, anagrams and relationships. As examples, two actual questions employed were:

1 Insert the word that means the same as the two words outside the brackets: Stake (....) mail
2 Which is the odd one out? Ofeed fstiw insietne tsuian dryah

The answers are (1) post and (2) Einstein (insietne) – the others are fiction authors.

With merely these examples it is easy to see the cultural requirements and the necessary type of knowledge in order to do well in such tests. The subjective nature of intelligence is apparent.

NATURE VERSUS NURTURE

One of the most important and yet contentious issues with regard to intelligence is how it originates in the first place. Is it a natural/programmed entity or is it something that is learnt through education and experience? Is it due to nature or is it due to nurture? Perhaps a more pertinent, and certainly more frequently asked, question is: in the make-up of an individual's intelligence, what percentage is inherited and what percentage can be put down to environmental effects through life?

The question is perhaps similar to asking: when baking a cake, how much of the quality of the cake is down to the original mix of ingredients and how much is down to how it is cooked? For the cake we would see both aspects as being important and the overall quality as being a subtle mixture of the two. Sometimes the cake might come out really well despite it not being left in the oven for an 'optimal' time, whereas sometimes it can turn out badly even when the recipe has been followed to the letter. What people have been looking for, for thousands of years (certainly back to Plato in third-century BC Greece), is the recipe for intelligence.

If we look back to the start of this chapter, at the Macmillan definition of intelligence, which included the ability to reason and profit from experience, we can see that it points to both inheritance and environment as contributing factors, although quite sensibly it doesn't make a stab at suggesting what the proportions are. In the past, the majority view has invariably swung one way or the other, often due to the political climate at the time.

For example, nineteenth-century western society was ordered strictly by class, the upper classes being considered (by the upper classes) to be more intelligent, the lower classes being considered as feeble-minded idiots. The general concept was that it was intelligence that had brought about such differences and through genetic inheritance the class structure was preserved.

In fact, Plato had taken the same approach 2,300 years earlier. He saw a person's intelligence as being class-related and felt that to maintain the status quo people should only produce offspring with members of their own class. At that time, average levels of intelligence were further maintained, so it was felt, by killing children at birth (or in infancy) if they were seen to display characteristics of 'idiocy'.

Only one century later, in Aristotle's time, things had changed. Levels of intelligence were then considered to be more dependent on teaching and life experience. Aristotle himself said that intelligence was present in all citizens. On the surface this may sound to be quite radical; however, it must be remembered that slaves, labourers, many women and most foreigners were all excluded from citizenship and therefore from being intelligent.

Approaching the present time, eighteenth-century philosophers such as John Stuart Mill strongly supported the nurture hypothesis, although they were generally outnumbered and outpoliticised by those whose ideas reflected inherited intelligence, which was deemed appropriate for the colonialism and capitalism of the time.

In the century that followed, Darwin's publication of *On the Origin of Species* (in 1859) regarding the means of natural selection led to huge support for the genetic nature of intelligence, which bolstered the idea of different levels of intelligence between nations, races, classes and individuals, thereby providing evidenced reasoning to justify slavery and oppression. It was also concluded that poorer people should be allowed to die out in order that society could maintain a higher average level of intelligence. This meant that poor people were not given social welfare and, in some parts of the world, were not even allowed to breed.

These days substantial research is focused on attempts to discover what percentage of intelligence in humans is produced by hereditary factors and what is due to the environment. Both genetics and education need to be considered. However, this is not easy. If a child from a poor background does not develop in terms of their intelligence as well as a child from a wealthy background, what is the reason? Is it because their genetic make-up is different or is it because they have not grown up in as stimulating an environment? Or rather, is it a complex relationship of both factors?

Some more recent studies have even put great emphasis on the environment before birth. A 1997 article in *Nature* claimed that foetal development in the womb accounted for 20% of an individual's total intelligence and that genetic influences only accounted for 34%, the remaining 46% being due to environmental factors after birth. While this study certainly has a basis of plausibility, the percentages are somewhat contrary to the norm − a straw poll of research papers indicate figures of 60–80% being down to inheritance with the remaining 40–20% being due to education and training.

An interesting study in Denmark looked at 100 men and women adopted in and around Copenhagen between 1924 and 1947. All the adoptees in the study had little in common with their biological siblings in terms of their environment and education, but shared a common environmental upbringing with their adoptive siblings. The results showed that, despite their upbringing, biologically related siblings closely resembled each other in terms of occupational status, whereas there was no significant correlation between adoptive siblings.

TWINS

One area of considerable interest is the study of identical twins – who can be deemed to have a pretty close genetic make-up of their brains – even including the period in the womb. Hence any perceived differences, so the theory goes, can be explained by nurture rather than nature.

In 1976, in a detailed study of 850 twins, John Loehlin came to the conclusion that the make-up of intelligence was something like 80/20 in favour of inheritance (nature) over environment (nurture). The particular group of twins who are of most interest, however, are those who have been separated at birth and who have been brought up in completely different environments.

In 1966 Cyril Burt presented results on over 53 pairs of identical twins who, he claimed, had been separated at birth, randomly placed in their adoptive homes and had no further contact with each other since birth. He came up with a figure of 86/14 in favour of nature over nurture, although it must be said that his results were subsequently discredited in terms of the validity of the twins used for the studies.

More recently, at the University of Minneapolis, a special unit was set up specifically for the study of twins, and many interesting statistics have subsequently been obtained. For example, results were pooled on a total of 122 pairs of identical twins in terms of IQ test scores. Similarities between pairs of twins correlated to be 82% (similar to the other results). However, unlike Burt's claimed study, twins tended to be brought up in similar home backgrounds due to that being the strategy of the social services responsible. In fact, results did not correlate so well for those twins who had grown up in dissimilar backgrounds.

As well as numerical pointers, a plethora of anecdotal 'evidence' has also been obtained. As an example (and this is just one of many), consider the twins Jim Springer and Jim Lewis. Both were adopted by separate Ohio families when only a few weeks old, and grew up completely independently in different towns until they met again at the age of 39. On meeting, they found that they drank the same brand of beer and smoked the same number of the same brand of cigarettes every day. Both men had a basement workshop and had built a circular bench, which they painted white, around a tree trunk. It continues: in their youth they both hated spelling but enjoyed mathematics and both had owned dogs which they called 'Toy'. When they left school, both men joined the local police force, got promoted to the rank of deputy sheriff and left after exactly seven years. Both men married and divorced women called Linda and then both married women called Betty, with whom they had one son, although Jim Lewis' child was named James Alan while Jim Springer's child was called James Allan. Both men took annual holidays in the same week at the same Florida beach, although somehow they never met up. After being brought together they both took an IQ test and gave almost identical answers. Of course, this could all be pure coincidence, but…

COMPARATIVE INTELLIGENCE

Intelligence in humans results from the functioning of their brain – their mental processing. What that person subjectively regards as being an intelligent act also results from that same mental processing. Within a group there tends to be a consensus agreement, dependent on culture, as to what is an intelligent act.

What an individual considers to be an intelligent act depends on what thought processes and skills they value. Such decisions are coloured by life experiences, culture and their mental processing, which exhibit a genetic influence. Individuals function as a part of some form of society; their intelligence is therefore of relevance to and determined by that particular society.

When taken out of the context of society, the concept of intelligence is relatively meaningless. Any value judgements or measurements are made in the context of an individual's cultural environment. The theoretical physicist Albert Einstein was not noted as a footballer and the footballer David Beckham might not be the best theoretical physicist, but in their own fields they have both excelled and have been regarded as intelligent. But what if Einstein's theories were overturned or Beckham broke his leg? Would they still be just as intelligent as they were? Would either of them be the best musician?

As we tend to apply subjective measurements between humans, so we do with other creatures and even machines. Because we are humans we can give value to things we do as humans – in a simplistic way it is then difficult to give value to what other creatures do unless they are merely mimicking what a human can do. We tend to relate everything to a human value set, including intelligence.

All creatures, including humans, have evolved as balanced entities, physical and mental processes working in harmony. A human's intelligence is part of their overall make-up and relates directly to their physical abilities. For each creature there exists a subjective intelligence which is relevant to their species and so further within a particular group of that species. Exactly the same is true with machines, in the broadest sense, in that subjective intelligence applies to particular skills and abilities that that type of machine exhibits.

It is clear that both mental and physical abilities are different between species. It is therefore extremely difficult to measure the performance of an individual in one species with an individual from another species, other than in the sense of performance in a specific task. We could, for example, consider the ability to cover a distance over land in a minimum time, comparing a cheetah, a human, an automobile and a snail. My guess is that the human might finish in the top three. But the result would only relate to one specific task – speed over a distance. We could also compare a human with a spider and a military tank in terms of web-making abilities – I'm not sure where humans would finish there as we do not have the physical capability to do so naturally.

Both of these tests could be regarded as very silly comparisons. But the same could easily be said if we compared a human, a rabbit and a computer in terms of ability to interact with a second human in a Chinese conversation. In fact, certain computers could well do a lot better than many humans (including myself) who cannot communicate at all in Chinese.

So, making a comparison between the abilities of individuals from different species is relatively meaningless other than in terms of the skills required to complete a particular task. This is particularly true when we wish to make comparisons between humans and machines in terms of aspects of intelligence. We really need to be clear which human or humans we are talking about and which machine or machines are being considered. Is the comparison being made in terms of a task that is extremely human centric?

Can we expect the machine to carry out a task in exactly the same way as a human? Indeed, is that at all relevant? Surely the end result is the critical thing, not how the machine performed? If one human plays another human at chess, both must abide by the rules of the game – this is obvious. The winner is not then disqualified because they were thinking about food when they were playing. So if a machine beats a human at chess we should not say: yes, but it wasn't thinking in exactly the same way as the human it beat, therefore it has lost.

CONCLUDING REMARKS

In this chapter we have tried to uncover what exactly intelligence is all about in order that we can move forward to look more deeply at AI. We have seen how intelligence is an integral part of an individual and that how the world is presented, in terms of sensing, and how the world is manipulated, in terms of motor abilities, are important factors that need to be taken into account.

It has been stressed as vitally important to consider intelligence in other creatures as well as humans and to look at intelligence in humans in terms of the broad spread of individuals that form humanity as a whole and not simply an 'ideal'. We will see, in our study of AI, that it is often tempting to compare the intellectual abilities of a machine with those of a human – in order perhaps to assess the standing of AI in relation to human intelligence. In doing so, we need to make sure that we do not make fools of ourselves in drawing conclusions that are relatively naïve.

We have considered here the make-up of human intelligence in terms of some aspects being due to nature and others due to nurture. With machines, of whatever type, it is much the same. There will be an initial design and build – which may include mechanical and/or biological components – and this may be subject to an initial program or arrangement – this is nature! Once the machine starts interacting with its environment and learning – in a variety of ways – then nurture can be seen to be having an effect. If a specific machine does not have the facility to learn, then (as would be the case for a human) it is extremely limited in what it can ultimately do. It is therefore assumed throughout this text that machines are subject to both nature and nurture.

We will start our investigation into AI by looking at its classical origins and see how some of the original systems were developed.

FURTHER READING

1   *Intelligence: A Very Short Introduction* by Ian J. Deary, published by Oxford Paperbacks, 2001. A good general introductory guide to human intelligence, for the non-specialist.

2   *On Intelligence* by J. Hawkins and S. Blakeslee, published by Owl Books, 2005. A look at how human brains work and how we measure intelligence in humans. It also takes a critical look at intelligence in machines and how this relates to the human form.

3   *QI: The Quest for Intelligence* by K. Warwick, published by Piatkus, 2000. This is a look at intelligence in humans, animals and machines, for the non-specialist. It tries to get to the bottom of just what intelligence actually is.

4   *Multiple Intelligences: New Horizons in Theory and Practice* by Howard Gardner, published by Basic Books, revised 2nd edition, 2006. This book considers human intelligence as separate human capacities, ranging from musical intelligence to the intelligence involved in understanding.

2

CLASSICAL AI

SYNOPSIS

Initial approaches to AI focused largely on classical, top-down methods which formed the first stages of the subject. In particular, knowledge-based systems and expert systems are considered here, especially the importance of the IF ... THEN ... statement. We consider how such statements can form a basic AI engine and how these can be applied for problem solutions. Both logic and fuzzy logic are discussed.

INTRODUCTION

It is undoubtedly a characteristic of humanity that we like to compare ourselves with others and, in many cases, try to find ways in which we are better than someone or something else. As computers began to appear on the scene and the concept of AI was born in the 1950s and 1960s, so the desire arose to directly compare AI with human intelligence. But with this comparison came a basic ground rule that human intelligence was as good as intelligence got, in some cases to the extent of believing that human intelligence was the only form of intelligence. It followed, therefore, that the best AI could achieve was to be as good as human intelligence and to copy it in some way.

So it transpired that classical AI techniques focused on getting a machine to copy human intelligence. This was borne out by an early definition from Marvin Minsky, who said: 'Artificial intelligence is the science of making machines do things that would require intelligence if done by men.' Quite neatly (and probably intentionally) this definition side-steps the whole concept of what intelligence is and what it is not and merely points to machines copying humans.

The philosophy of that time is perhaps best described by a statement made by Herb Simon in 1957, who was quoted as saying: 'There are now in the world machines that think, that learn and that create. Moreover, their ability to do these things is going to increase rapidly until ... the range of problems they can handle will be coextensive with the range to which the human mind has been applied.'

What arose in those days was an approach to AI rather along the lines of a psychiatrist: attempting to understand the human brain's processing merely from the outside and then attempting to build a machine to copy that way of functioning – a top-down approach.

One aspect of human intelligence that was picked up on in those days was the ability of the human brain to reason. If given a number of facts the human brain can make a reasoned assumption about a situation and decide on a conclusion. For example, if it is 7 a.m. and my alarm clock is ringing then it is time to get up. It was this approach that was first used successfully to build AI systems.

EXPERT SYSTEMS

The concept of an expert system is that of a machine being able to reason about facts in a specific domain and to work in roughly the same way that an expert's brain would work. To do this the machine would need knowledge about that domain, some rules (generated by experts) to follow when new information occurred and some way of communicating with a user of the overall system. Such systems are called rule-based systems, knowledge-based systems or, more generally, expert systems.

One of the first successful working systems was called MYCIN, which was a medical system to diagnose blood infections. MYCIN contained approximately 450 rules and was claimed to be better than many junior doctors and as good as some experts. It had no theoretically generated rules but rather was built up by interviewing large numbers of experts who could report from direct experience. The rules could therefore, partially at least, reflect the uncertainties apparent with medical conditions.

The general structure of MYCIN was similar to that of all expert systems. In an expert system, each rule is of the basic form:

IF (condition) THEN (conclusion).

For example, a rule in MYCIN could be IF (sneezing) THEN (flu).

However, it may be that several conditions must exist at the same time for a condition to be apparent (for the rule to be true) or, conversely, one of a number of conditions could exist in order that a conclusion can be drawn. So, it may be that a rule looks more like:

IF (condition1 and condition2 or condition3) THEN (conclusion).

In the medical example this might become:

IF (sneezing and coughing or headache) THEN (flu).

The actual rules employed are obtained by questioning a number of experts as to their opinion. In this case it was medical experts: what are the symptoms of flu? Or, if a patient is sneezing and coughing what does this mean?

It might be that there are several possible conclusions that can be drawn from the same set of facts. This would be a problem for an expert just as it is for an expert system. In order to deal with such a situation, the system has to have further rules purely for such instances in order to decide what course of action to take – this is referred to as conflict resolution.

CONFLICT RESOLUTION

There are many situations in which several conditions are met but that only one conclusion is required. In such cases a decision is necessary as to which of the rules (all of which have conditions that have been fully met) takes precedence. The conflict between these rules must be resolved. There are a number of possibilities; the actual one to be employed depends on the expert system itself. When several rules have all their conditions met, the one selected depends on one of the following criteria being applied:

1   Highest priority rule – each rule has a priority associated with it and if several rules apply, the one with the highest priority is chosen.
2   Highest priority conditions – each condition has a priority associated with it. For a rule to be chosen it must contain the highest priority conditions.
3   Most recent – the rule whose condition has most recently been met is chosen.
4   Most specific – the rule which has most conditions met is selected. This is also referred to as 'longest matching'.
5   Context limiting – rules are split into groups, only some of which are active at a certain time. To be chosen a rule must belong to an active group – in this way the expert system can adapt over time to different conditions.

Which conflict resolution method is employed depends entirely on the application – for simple systems the resolution itself will most likely be very simple.

In certain circumstances the expert system may be expected to draw several conclusions from the same set of conditions, and may merely be required to inform the user that these conditions all apply at that time. Any further decisions, and hence any conflict resolution, can then be carried out by the user.

MULTIPLE RULES

Most expert systems involve several rules which depend on each other. These are structured in layers. Hence, when all the conditions are met for one rule such that its conclusion is drawn, that conclusion can in turn meet a condition for a rule in the next layer, and so on. As an example, consider an engine management system for a vehicle:

Layer 1 Rules:
IF (start button pressed) THEN (start engine)
IF (gear selection made) THEN (engage gears)

Layer 2 Rule:
IF (engine started and gears engaged) THEN (vehicle drive)

It is clear that both layer 1 rules must have fired in order that both conditions are met for the layer 2 rule to fire such that the vehicle can drive. It could be considered that the condition for rule 2 to fire has become a fact because both necessary rules in layer 1 have fired. There is, of course, no conflict resolution required in this case as the rules are independent.

It is obvious from this example, however, that if we include other factors such as brakes depressed, minimum fuel level in the tank, direction selected, object in front of the vehicle and so on, the expert system rapidly becomes more complex, with many layers of rules dealing with often conflicting requirements. It is interesting to consider the total number of rules that would be necessary for an expert system to drive a vehicle on the normal road network.

In this case the original facts (data) entering our expert system are: first, the start button has been pressed; and second, that the gear selection has been made. Further facts are then realised in that the engine starts and the gears are engaged. Subsequently, the overall goal is realised as the vehicle drives. So we start with a set of facts which are input to our expert system and a goal which is achieved, which could be said to be the output.

FORWARD CHAINING

With an expert system in normal operation, a set of facts will be apparent at a particular time and these will fire a number of rules, realising further facts which fire other rules and so on until an end conclusion is reached, much as has been described in the engine management example. This way of working from the input data to the end goal is referred to as 'forward chaining'. The purpose is to discover all that can be deduced from a given set of facts.

BACKWARD CHAINING

Expert systems can also be used in a reverse fashion. In this sense, when a goal has been achieved the rules are then searched to investigate what facts (data) occurred in order for the system to reach the conclusion that it did. It is also possible to look backwards through the system to assess what facts we must input to the system in order for a specific goal to be realised.

In the given example, the question could be asked: what happened to cause the vehicle to drive? Backward chaining would then be employed to provide the answer that the start button was pressed and the gear selection had been made.

Backward chaining is good for system verification, particularly where the expert system must be safety critical and cannot arrive at a 'wrong' conclusion. It is also useful to assess the overall performance of the system in order to find out if further rules are necessary or if a strange set of (input) circumstances can cause an unexpected conclusion to be drawn.

GOOD POINTS

Expert systems have a number of advantages over other AI methods.

First, it can be seen that they are fairly easy to programme into a computer (uniform lines of code in an IF–THEN structure). Each rule is a separate entity with its own required data to fire and its own individual conclusion drawn. If a new rule is deemed necessary it can be added to the overall system, although sometimes this might mean also altering rules governing conflict resolution.

The system is ideal for dealing with natural real-world information. After all, it is the same information dealt with by experts. So when an expert says 'in such a situation this is what I do', this can readily be entered into the expert system.

The system structure is separate from the data, and hence the problem area, in the sense that the same expert system structure could be employed in very different domains. It is merely the rules themselves and how they are combined that would differ. Hence the same expert system structure in a computer could be used for the medical diagnosis system as well as the engine management system, although different rules would need to be entered, different data would cause the rules to fire and different conclusions would be drawn.

An expert system can deal with uncertainty, as we will see when we consider fuzzy logic. In this case, when a series of facts are presented the conclusion of the system might be that, given those facts, it is 75% certain about the conclusion it is drawing. This may well be indicative of other useful evidence that is missing that could otherwise make the system 100% certain. Medical diagnosis is one example where confidence values are useful. Given the symptoms input as facts, the expert system could give an output which indicates that it is only 50% sure of the diagnosis. In such a situation the experts themselves are rarely (if ever) 100% certain about a diagnosis – this is merely reflected in the system itself.

One big advantage of such a system, as with most AI systems, is speed of response, especially when compared to the speed of a human expert. When the last piece of necessary information arrives it may take only a small fraction of a second for the machine to come to its conclusion. A human expert may take several seconds or, in some circumstances, many minutes to arrive at the same conclusion for the same problem. This could mean significant financial savings or that the safety of individuals is enhanced. Expert systems to deal with machine or supply failure alarms or financial dealing systems are excellent examples.

PROBLEMS WITH EXPERT SYSTEMS

There are a number of problems with expert systems. First, gathering the rules can prove to be rather awkward. Often it is difficult for a person to put into simple terms what it is they do in an everyday situation. On top of this, if several experts are asked, they may well think about the problem in different ways, such that it is difficult to standardise the rules. This may mean that they differ completely on a solution. In some cases it may be possible to average results, but in other cases it may not. Consider, for example, an expert system designed to drive a vehicle: in the situation of an object directly in front, one expert may suggest steering to the left while another may prefer steering to the right. Averaging these responses and steering directly ahead would not be sensible!

It is also worth pointing out that human experts, particularly specialists, can be quite expensive, particularly if several of them are needed, and it can be problematic to book them up and obtain answers from them. All this time and expense goes towards the cost of realising the overall system.

One of the biggest problems with expert systems is what is referred to as 'combinatorial explosion'. Quite simply, the expert system becomes too big. One main aim of such a system is to deal with problems and to draw a conclusion no matter what the situation. But in order to deal with absolutely every eventuality, rules must be continually added to cover every possible situation, no matter how unlikely. As an example, consider the case of the expert system to drive a vehicle on normal roads: it is unlikely that an elephant will walk in front of the vehicle, it is unlikely there will be lots of mud and it is unlikely there will be a settee, but there may be and the rules must take care of each of these circumstances.

Because some expert systems may contain many thousands of rules, even to deal with something that may, to a human, be relatively straightforward, at each occurrence many (if not all) of these rules must be tested, along with any necessary conflict resolution and chaining. So rather than being much faster than a human expert, when many rules are present such a system may well be much slower than a human in making a decision. Debugging such a system to ensure that it works in each and every eventuality can also be difficult, with rules interacting and possibly cancelling each other out.

One final point to make here is that expert systems are merely one type of AI, being indicative of simply one aspect of intelligence in general. In particular, they attempt to mimic the reasoning function of the human brain in terms of how decisions are reached given a number of facts at a particular time, based on expert knowledge about what to do with those facts.

It is important not to see such systems as merely programmed decision-making mechanisms that will always perform as we expect. It is certainly possible to operate them in this way, but it is also possible to enable them to learn as they draw conclusions and experience their domain. Clearly this depends on the function for which they are required. Such learning will be considered in greater detail later.

Suffice here to say that if such a system draws a number of conclusions then the rules which resulted in the 'winning/selected' conclusion can be 'rewarded' in the sense of making them more likely to fire and/or be part of the overall conclusion next time around. Conversely, if a fired rule results in a conclusion which is not chosen then it will be less likely to fire again. Success is rewarded and failure is punished! This could also be achieved through prioritising for conflict resolution.

FUZZY LOGIC

With the expert systems we have considered thus far in this chapter it has been assumed that either a condition exists or it doesn't. This is straightforward logic. A fact is either true or false.

Yet, as we saw, it was found useful in certain circumstances for conclusions to be partially true or rather for a confidence percentage to be applied to results. Indeed, this is how many things in human life actually appear. If someone is having a shower they want the water to be warm. The water is not simply hot or cold, it is warm. Fuzzy logic provides a basis for this.

Let us assume for a moment that for shower water to be completely cold it will be at a temperature of 0°C, whereas for it to be completely hot it will be at a temperature of 50°C. If the actual water we are measuring has a temperature between 0°C and 50°C then we can say, for example, that it is 65% hot, meaning that it is fairly warm, but has some way to go before it is hot. If it is 12% hot, then it is pretty cold.

Although I have given the shower water values as percentages, using fuzzy logic does not necessarily mean that the actual measured temperature would be 65% of 50°C (32.5°C). Fuzzy logic is more directed to a human concept of the temperature – remember it is a form of AI. So we can, if we wish, draw up a relationship between the actual temperature and the percentage value we will assign it, between 0% and 100%.

FUZZIFICATION

In a fuzzy logic system the first step is to take an actual real-world value and make it fuzzy – this is referred to as 'fuzzification'. If we are dealing with the temperature of water, the actual water temperature would be measured and then fuzzified. For example, a temperature of 20°C might become a fuzzy value of 45%. This fuzzy value can then be input to our fuzzy expert system.

The relationship between the actual value and fuzzy value needs to be well defined for a particular problem – this could be done through graphical means or possibly a look-up table or even through mathematical relationships. As an example we could have, for our water temperature, the following:

0°C becomes 0%, 10°C becomes 20% – in between add 2% for every 1°C, so 3°C would become 6%.
10°C becomes 20% and 30°C becomes 80% – in between add 3% for every 1°C, so 24°C would become 62%.
30°C becomes 80% and 50°C becomes 100% – in between add 1% for every 1°C, so 43°C would become 93%.

The actual fuzzification routine depends entirely on the particular application. This example has merely been given to show what is possible.

FUZZY RULES

Once a value has been fuzzified it is passed to the rules for evaluation. Fuzzy rules are the same as those we have already seen:

IF (condition) THEN (conclusion)

However, we now have the situation that the condition may be only partially true. For an expert system in which the water is either hot or cold, we may have had the rules:

IF (water is cold) THEN (turn water heater on)
IF (water is hot) THEN (turn water heater off)

Now we can replace these rules with one fuzzy rule:

> IF (water is hot) THEN (turn water heater on)

This may appear strange at first glance, but it must be remembered that we are dealing with fuzzy rules – so the condition part will be a percentage value (not simply 'yes' or 'no'). As a consequence, the conclusion part will also be a percentage value. Now the water heater will not simply be turned on or off, but will be turned on to a certain extent – as we will see.

As we saw before, with straightforward expert systems, it may be that a rule has several conditions that need to be satisfied before the rule can fire, or conversely any one of a number of conditions might occur for a rule to fire. For example:

> IF (water is hot AND energy tariff is high) THEN (turn water heater on)

This would require both conditions to be true for the water heater to turn on. Alternatively:

> IF (water is cold OR energy tariff is low) THEN (turn water heater on)

This would require either (or both) of the conditions to be true for the water heater to turn on.

But with fuzzy rules, each of the conditions has a percentage assigned to it. Most fuzzy systems operate as follows. Where the AND term appears the *minimum* percentage value of the condition is carried forward. Where the OR term appears the *maximum* percentage value of the condition is carried forward.

As an example, we might have the fuzzy rule:

> IF (water temperature is hot AND energy tariff is high)
> THEN (turn water heater on)

For this example, let's imagine that after fuzzification the water temperature has been assigned a value of 62% and the (also fuzzified) energy tariff has been assigned a value of 48%. The value carried forward, as this is an AND operation, will be the minimum of the values 62% and 48% – i.e. it will be 48%. Conversely, if the condition contained an OR operation then the value taken forward would be the maximum of the values involved, in this case 62%. We will see shortly what happens with the value taken forward.

It may be that only one rule fires in an expert system; however, it is more normally the case that a number of different rules will fire. Each of the rules will then result in a different value taken forward and these values must be aggregated to provide a single end value that means something in the outside world. In the example we are considering here, we require an overall percentage output which will indicate how much the water heater needs to be turned on.

DEFUZZIFICATION

There are a number of ways in which the different percentage values taken forward can be aggregated. Perhaps the simplest, and most obvious, is merely to average the values.

If we have three rules – R1, R2 and R3 – which have produced the resultant percentage values R1 = 23%, R2 = 81% and R3 = 49%, then the average value would be the three percentages added together and divided by three (i.e. 51%). In our example, this refers to how much the water heater must be turned on – just over half way.

However, as discussed previously it is often the case that some rules will be more important that others. The most typical defuzzification method is therefore a weighted average method – referred to as the 'centre of gravity' (COG) method. In this case each resultant percentage value is multiplied by an associated weighting value, the answers being added together and divided by the total of all the weighting values added together.

In the example just considered let us assume that R1 is more important than the others, so we'll give it a weighting of 5; R2 gets a weighting of 2; and R3 a weighting of 3. R2 is therefore the least important of the rules. When we add these weights together the answer is 10. Now we multiply our values for R1–R3 by their weighting (23×5, 81×2 and 49×3), the result of which is 424, which, when we divide it by 10 (the sum of the weights we applied) gives us a defuzzified value of 42.4%. This is lower than the previous unweighted calculation because more emphasis, through the weighting, was placed on the output of rule R1 which was much lower than the outputs of the other two rules. Because of this the water would not be heated to the same extent.

FUZZY EXPERT SYSTEM

In building an expert system it is simply the case that rules must be generated and arranged in layers with an appropriate conflict resolution scheme put in place.

With fuzzy expert systems we certainly need rules, but in this case they must be fuzzy rules. It may be that a conflict resolution scheme is also necessary; however, this may well not be so as the defuzzification technique can, in this case, take into account things such as prioritisation between the rules and can even reflect the time that a rule fires by making the defuzzification weighting values time-dependent. As an example, when a fuzzy rule first fires its relative weighting value might be high, but as time passes the weighting might diminish with respect to time. This can be to the extent that if a particular rule has not fired for a long time, it is weighted as zero, i.e. it will be ignored by the system. So even if a rule has fired, when a certain period of time has elapsed, it can be overlooked in the defuzzification routine.

In the case of fuzzy expert systems, as well as a set of fuzzy rules, also required are appropriate fuzzification and defuzzification schemes. Defuzzification needs to take into account what the output value is actually intended for – possibly controlling a motor or pump to a proportion of its full capabilities or maybe driving a vehicle at a percentage of its full speed.

Fuzzification can be more problematic as the different quantities being fuzzified can be very different terms in reality, such as voltages, temperature or flow rate, which are all measured differently. Unfortunately, there is not really a well-defined, tried-and-tested systematic way to build up either the fuzzification method or the subsequent fuzzy rules. Hence, in order to obtain a successful fuzzy expert system quite a bit of trial and error is necessary to obtain the best performance.

PROBLEM SOLVING

We have looked at one aspect of AI in which we can enter a set of rules for the system to follow, such that all eventualities are covered. A different type of situation occurs when we need to realise an AI system to solve problems for us. One simple example of this exists in a satellite navigation system as used for vehicle guidance. We (hopefully) know where our start point is and we also know where we wish to get to, but we don't know how to get there.

This is rarely a trivial problem as many different solutions exist. So it is usually the case that we have further requirements, such as wishing to know the quickest route or possibly the shortest one, or we could even require the most scenic route – in fact, there are all sorts of potential requirements when travelling from place to place. This type of problem is typical of many and is something that AI can be very good at solving – very quickly.

Let's assume that we wish to travel from the town of Reading to Newcastle via several other towns. There are many possible routes to take. For example, we could start by travelling from Reading to Oxford or possibly Reading to London. Both of those routes would have costs associated with them in terms of the time the route would take, the fuel used, the distance travelled and so on. From Oxford one could travel to Banbury or possibly Stratford and so on; each path from one town to the next has costs associated with it. Finally, the end goal of Newcastle is reached.

On the assumptions that we limit the number of possible towns to be considered on our trip from Reading to Newcastle and that we only visit a town once, then there are a number of ways that an AI system could search for the best solution.

BREADTH-FIRST SEARCH

In order to decide which is the best solution to our travel problem, it is necessary to consider all possibilities. In our example with Reading as a start point we could search for the best route by first looking at all the possible towns to travel to from Reading – Oxford and London included. For each of those towns we could then look at all the possible choices from them. At each stage we would evaluate the total cost of taking that route.

We would eventually arrive at Newcastle via a number of different routes, but as we have a record of the total cost of each of these routes, a comparison could be made between them to decide which is best in terms of distance, time or whatever is the requirement. Essentially, we would have looked at all possible solutions and after making a comparison, as long as the costing information was accurate, we would definitely be able to find the best solution.

In some cases, particularly for simple routes with only a few towns, such a search is perfectly acceptable. However, because of the number of potential solutions it can prove to be problematic in terms both of the amount of computer memory required and the time taken, even on a very powerful computer, for all routes to be considered and associated costs calculated. The memory problem is caused by the fact that all information about all routes must be saved until we reach the goal town of Newcastle, when the final comparison can be made.

DEPTH-FIRST SEARCH

In a depth-first search, one complete route is tried initially from the start point to finish at the goal. Then a different route is tried from start to finish. Immediately a cost comparison can be made between the two and the best one retained. Other routes can be systematically tried in the same way. If we are only looking for the best solution then only one route needs to be retained in memory. If, on comparison, another route is found to be better in terms of cost (assuming this is our focus), then that simply replaces the original. For this type of search, computer memory requirements are therefore of little significance.

One big issue with depth-first searches is that if a poor initial choice is made, it can produce a direction that results in a very long and expensive path involving hundreds of towns. Other similar poor, long, paths may well then be searched next. Meanwhile, it might be that the best solution only involved starting in a different initial direction such that low-cost routes could be taken. With depth-first searches such a solution might not be discovered for some time. A breadth-first search, for the same problem, would have found such a solution very quickly.

DEPTH-LIMITED SEARCH

The problem of a depth-first search looking into extremely long and costly routes can be alleviated by a depth-limited search. A defined number of towns, the depth limit, on a journey is first selected. The search then commences in depth-first fashion until the defined number is reached. That particular search is given up on and the next one started in depth-first mode.

Clearly, an amount of common sense and, where possible, knowledge of the particular problem needs to be applied with a depth-limited search. The previous two techniques (breadth-first and depth-first) are known as 'blind searches' because little needs to be known about the problem for the search to go ahead. With a depth-limited search it would be stupid, for example, to choose a very low limit when the solution might be expected to produce a result of two or three steps. A brief study of the problem may well tell us that a solution is likely in, say, nine or ten steps, so a good choice for the limit in this case might be 10–11 – if a solution doesn't look good after that number of steps it is very unlikely to be the best solution, so let's give up and try another path.

BIDIRECTIONAL SEARCH

An alternative strategy is to split the search in two and to commence one search (forwards) from the start point and simultaneously to commence a second search (backwards) from the goal. The big advantage of this technique is that it can save a lot of time in finding a solution; however, it can require significant memory.

In order to succeed, as part of one of the searches, a routine must also be included to check on whether or not a point reached has also just been reached on the fringe of the other search. Knowledge of the problem is therefore useful here, as such a fringe-checking exercise, which can be time consuming, does not need to be carried out until such a depth has been reached that a solution is either likely or possible.

SEARCHING PROBLEMS

One enormous potential time waste is to repeatedly explore points that have already been reached and fully explored. This can result in never finding a solution or concluding with a poor or incorrect solution. For some problems (particularly simple ones) such a situation should not occur, but other problems can be complex and there may be several intermingling routes to consider.

To explain the problem in a little more detail, consider again attempting to travel from Reading to Newcastle. We may take one path from Reading to Oxford then on to Coventry, and subsequently explore all the possibilities from Coventry. As part of the search we may then try Reading to Banbury then on to Coventry – having arrived at Coventry by a different route. All possible paths out of Coventry, with their associated costs, have already been searched, so there is no point doing the same exercise again. However, it does mean that memory of all the different paths, with associated costs, is required until an overall solution has been found.

As part of the search it is necessary, when a new point is reached, to compare the point with those that have already been expanded. Apart from not expanding the point again, the two routes to that point can be compared, the best one selected and the loser discarded. As with intelligence in general, an AI search that forgets or ignores its past is likely to make the same mistakes over and over again.

PRACTICAL SEARCH EXAMPLES

Although a travelling example has been given here to explain some of the principles, the searching techniques described can be applied to find the solution to puzzles. One example is a Rubik's cube, where the initial start point is usually a random assortment of coloured squares on different faces of the cube, the end goal being when each of the faces of the cube consists of squares of only one colour.

Breaking down the problem, it is best to find a state that the cube can be in from which a known solution exists to reach the problem, and then a further state back from that, and so on. At any point in time it is then merely a case of taking a small step to get from one state to another, and thereby to reach the goal.

Maze-solving is another example, in this case where a human would typically use a depth-first strategy when a breadth-first strategy would most likely be much better. In fact, for a maze as encountered in a puzzle book the best strategy is almost surely a bidirectional search – working backwards from the goal as well as forwards. Unfortunately this usually makes the problem trivial and spoils all the fun.

In Jerome K. Jerome's *Three Men in a Boat*, Harris' solution to finding the centre of Hampton Court Maze was 'it's very simple ... you keep on taking the first turning on the right'. Unfortunately this resulted in his party repeatedly returning to the same point, to the extent that 'some of the people stopped and waited for the others [Harris] to walk round and come back to them'.

At a more complex level, games such as chess present themselves as prime examples. The present state at any time is the situation on the chess board, and the goal is to achieve checkmate. The added complexity in this case arises from the uncertainty as to what the opponent is likely to do. At any instant in time, therefore, the search must include costings that are based on probabilities rather than fixed values. So, unlike the travelling problem in which (traffic jams excluded) costs are assumed to be pretty much fixed, in chess the likely response of the opponent must be taken into account as much as possible.

In May 1997 the IBM computer Deep Blue beat the erstwhile human world chess champion, Garry Kasparov, over a six-match series. The computer was capable of extensively searching and analysing 200 million positions every second – thereby indicating a distinct advantage of AI over human intelligence in terms of speed of calculations. Kasparov said at the time: 'There were many, many discoveries in this match, and one of them was that sometimes the computer plays very, very human moves. It deeply understands positional factors.'

HEURISTIC SEARCHING

If some information is already held about the problem then different strategies exist to modify the search procedures as described. The actual technique used in any particular case depends very much on the nature of information held. One obvious method, referred to as a **best first search**, expands the search from a particular point based on the minimum expected cost of a solution. This can be extended, where cost estimations or probabilities need to be made, to finding the minimum of a mathematical function in which estimates of costs are drawn up for different solutions.

A **greedy best first search** merely expands the search by finding the minimum cost for the next step taken. This does not always produce the best solution but it is generally efficient and can be very quick.

Other techniques involve finding a list of all possible solutions and starting with one initial solution. This solution is then only dropped in order to select an alternative if the overall cost is better, which, in turn, is retained until it is bettered. This is generally referred to as **hill climbing** or **steepest descent**. It is what is referred to as a **local search** method as the list of solutions will be ordered such that similar solutions lie near to each other, with small changes being made to each solution. One problem of the technique therefore is that it will find the best solution which is only the best locally to those solutions around it – in other words, it may not find the overall (global) best solution. This is referred to as 'getting stuck in a local minimum'. Ways of getting around this involve randomly jumping to another part of the solution list.

KNOWLEDGE REPRESENTATION

One important aspect of the types of AI systems we are looking at here is how information or knowledge about the problem faced is stored and dealt with. Essentially, we have to decide what content to put in the knowledge base and how best to represent the world at large within a computer. In particular, we are faced with very different requirements depending on the type of information we are storing.

We must deal with the likes of physical objects, time, actions and beliefs we hold to be true in all sorts of different environments. Trying to model and represent everything in the world would be quite a significant task – humans cannot do this so we cannot expect an AI system to do so. But what can be represented is a limited domain of knowledge, focusing on a specific area or topic of interest.

There are several different approaches used in the world of AI to represent knowledge. Here we will look at one of the most widely used, a method called **frames**. Frames are used to represent large amounts of general purpose, **common sense knowledge**, in a structured way.

FRAMES

A frame represents necessary everyday typical knowledge about an entity. It is a file within the computer, with a number of pieces of information stored in slots in the file. Each of those slots is itself a sub-frame (or sub-file) with further embedded levels of information.

Let us assume that we have a frame-based AI system which is being used to describe a house. The initial frame is the house. Within the house are a number of slots, e.g. dining room, kitchen, lounge, etc. Each of these slots is then itself a frame. So we have a kitchen frame which contains a number of slots, e.g. refrigerator, cooker, sink, etc. These slots are, in turn, frames in themselves with slots of their own. And so on until a sufficient depth of knowledge is realised for the problem at hand.

Exactly the same basis is used for actions, with each potential action being described by a frame with slots containing sub-actions. If we had a frame for going outside, this might contain action slots such as put on shoes, put on coat, take car keys, etc. As you can see, this type of knowledge representation is very much like the way humans might think. If I am going outside, what must I remember to do?

Sometimes in everyday life, if the task we are faced with is unusual or is some time in the future, it is likely that we (as humans) might forget some of the slots. So we write down a list of what we need to do in order to accomplish the task. This list is essentially the principle of a frame-based knowledge store in an AI system.

A frame can contain (in its slots) all sorts of different pieces of information pertaining to the subject of the frame. These can be facts about, or objects within, a situation. Conversely, they could be knowledge about procedures or actions to be carried out. On the other hand, a frame could contain a mixture of this information.

If a frame describes an action then some of its slots describe the sub-tasks to be performed in order to carry out the overall action. But there also needs to be an actor slot, to indicate who or what is to carry out the action. It is also necessary for there to be an object slot, to indicate what or who will be acted upon; a source slot to indicate the start point; and a destination slot to describe the end point destination for this action.

METHODS AND DEMONS

Thus far we have seen how knowledge can be dealt with in the frame method. However, to employ this within an AI system we need to be able to manipulate and interrogate the knowledge. Methods and demons are the way in which appropriate actions can be carried out.

A method is a series of commands that is associated with a particular entity in a slot either to find out something about the entity or to carry out a series of actions when the value of the entity changes in a certain way. Methods can either be of the type *when changed* or *when needed*.

In a 'when changed' method, the appropriate procedure will be carried out when the value of the entity changes. For example, in a share-trading AI system, the value of a particular company's shares could be monitored. When it changes a procedure is then automatically carried out to test whether the share value is now above or below previously set threshold figures. If the value has gone outside these bounds then the shares may be automatically sold or bought as appropriate.

In a 'when needed' method, the appropriate procedure will be carried out when a request appears to find out what the value of the entity is. In our share-price example, at the time of a 'when needed' request, possibly from a potential investor, the value of the company's shares will be determined.

Demons are IF (condition) THEN (conclusion) statements which are fired when the value of the condition term changes. In this way demons and 'when changed' methods are very similar.

There are distinct similarities between expert systems – of the rule-based type considered earlier in this chapter – and the mode of operation of a frame system in terms of its methods and demons. Indeed, it is quite possible to operate a frame-based expert system.

The differences between the methods are slight and it is more down to the philosophy behind each approach. In a frame system the frames try to match to the present situation, the aim of the reasoning process carried out is then to find which frames apply at any time, i.e. which situation, action or object is the focus. If there is no match then another frame is given control, the attention is pointed elsewhere. A piece of data or value could change, but if it is nothing to do with the frame in control then it may have no impact.

A rule-based expert system is usually much more data driven. If a value changes then it may fire some rules which will create conclusions which could fire further rules, and so on. However, by employing conflict resolution, priorities can be set and this can effectively block certain rules from having any effect at certain times – which results in a similar method to a frame system. It must be pointed out, however, that for practical AI systems, a rule-based expert system is much more widely encountered, particularly within an industrial environment.

MACHINE LEARNING

One of the biggest misconceptions many people hold about computers is that they are unable to learn and adapt to new opportunities. It is certainly true that this may be the case for some computers in that they are merely programmed and are expected to perform only as they have been programmed. However, many computers can learn from experience, significantly alter their mode of operation and change their behaviour in fundamental ways. Of course, they must have been given the ability to do so, but do so they can.

In fact, an important aspect of the field of AI is the ability of computers to learn. With the classical types of AI that have been considered in this chapter, while they are perhaps not as well suited as some of the methods described in later chapters to adapting, other than through human input, they are nevertheless quite capable of doing so.

A rule-based expert system is, by definition, originally set up by extracting a series of rules from human experts, along with other pieces of information, e.g. data sheets on the problem domain.

What is produced is a bank of rules, some of which lead on to other rules when they fire. So upon certain data being input, a winning series of rules may involve 6, 7 or more rules firing in series, each one triggering the next to fire until the final conclusion of the final rule is reached. It follows that for an end rule to draw a conclusion, all the previous rules in the series needed to fire.

It may be that the conclusion drawn is a good one, as far as any action taken in the outside world is concerned – maybe shares are sold and a profit is made or perhaps an alarm is sounded in good time. Each of the rules that have taken part in the successful conclusion can then be rewarded such that when a similar set of input data occurs, the rules are even more likely to fire. This reward mechanism can be brought about either through prioritising via conflict resolution or by increasing condition percentage values in a fuzzy rule-based system. The opposite is true if the end conclusion turned out to be a bad one, whereby the rules are punished by decreasing probabilities.

The general method used is referred to as a **bucket brigade technique**, because the reward or punishment is passed back, in some measure, from the output conclusion. The method employed, the weightings applied and the amount of flexibility involved in the rules is all dependent on the problem domain. It may be, for example, that some rules must necessarily not change for safety or reliability reasons and these can then take no part in the learning process.

It is also possible for the computer to generate new rules by itself. A new rule can be brought about simply by allowing small mutations to the condition probabilities or the conflict resolution procedure. If the new rule then takes part in a successful end conclusion it will receive a reward and will strengthen. If, however, it takes part in any unsuccessful conclusions it will be punished on each occasion until it withers away. How much of this learning is allowed depends entirely on the problem and how much trial and error is allowed in the real world.

DATA MINING

Humans operate by obtaining facts, termed data, about the world around us and making informed, reasoned choices based on that information. This may be simply deciding which loaf of bread to buy based on the price or which train to catch depending on timing and venue. However, the extent of information available to us now is, for many decisions, far more than our human brains can cope with – it's a case of information overload. Hence many companies exist simply to advise us, at a price, as to, for example, which insurance to purchase and how to go about it. We rely on them to do the 'difficult' thinking for us.

Even when buying a simple product we are faced with a plethora of different types of data. Different suppliers, prices and products with different performance measures, insurance deals, delivery offers and so on. We don't want to make a fool of ourselves and waste our time and money. However, we would like to get that special deal, a bargain because we had the right advice at the right time.

Whether it is carried out by a human or a machine, extracting vital pieces of knowledge from the complexity of available data on a particular topic is referred to as data mining. AI systems are well suited to this because of their ability to store enormous quantities of data and to draw out all sorts of relationships within that data in order to realise patterns, connections and links that are meaningful.

It is said that the amount of data in the world (approximately) doubles each year – this means that over a ten-year period (e.g. 2002 to 2012) there is a 1,000 times increase in data! Many new areas of study arise because of improvements in technology, and each of these inputs significantly to the data available – data that are not well understood and often with meanings that are not readily drawn out. In recent years the Human Genome Project has opened up the complexities of DNA, and now we are able to look into the functioning of brains (even human brains) and try to make sense of what is going on based on the new forms of data obtained. There are, as a result, new business opportunities to seize, new medical techniques to develop and, most important of all, a more in-depth understanding of the scientific world around us is available. But we need to understand the data collected.

CORRELATIONS

There are a lot of situations in which many different pieces of data exist. What we may wish to discover are similarities, links and relationships between these pieces. Or, it may be that we wish to discover the most important pieces. On the other hand, it is possible that we wish to predict likely outcomes in the future based on the data available to this time – so we need to know which pieces of data are useful for the prediction and which are not.

One example is supermarket shopping. For many people such shopping is a regular exercise, e.g. the main weekly shop is carried out every Thursday evening. There are approximately 100 different types of produce available in a typical (mainly food) supermarket, and every time such a person uses the supermarket, data is obtained on what they have purchased.

Over a period of time statistical links can then be drawn up for an individual as to what they buy and how often they buy it. Similarly for the different products, links can be drawn from the data to indicate which people buy certain products and when they buy them. A clear aim here is to be able to say: 'Next Thursday a certain person will enter the supermarket, they will buy this product and that product – if we make them available the person will also buy other products based on our predictions.' The prediction may not be 100% accurate for a particular person at a particular time, but over 100 or 1,000 people it may well be sufficiently accurate (on average) for a significant profit to be made. This is how profit can be made from data mining.

One basic statistical technique that can be applied is that of correlation – to see how one piece of data is linked to another piece of data. As an example, let's consider our person visiting the supermarket over a period of one year, and look at their purchases of milk and cheese. The data on how much milk and cheese was purchased by that person, week by week, over the one-year period can then be analysed to see how the two pieces of data are related to each other. When one increases does the other increase, when one decreases does the other? A number of statistical tools are available for this, such as Principal Component Analysis, which detects the main links between different pieces of data, e.g. for one person the purchasing of shoe polish may be closely linked to buying pickles. But using a computer this analysis can be carried out for all 100 (or more) different products.

Such techniques have been used to discover many strange facts about regular purchasing patterns in supermarkets. One intriguing example is the link, particularly on Friday nights, for young male adults to purchase both nappies (diapers) and beer – I will leave you to draw your own conclusions about this!

DECISION TREES

One technique used to reduce the complexity of problems, and hence to make an enormous database a little easier to analyse, is the use of decision trees. It is essentially a method whereby the entire database is chopped up into more manageable proportions, based on the requirements of the user. This makes it easy to follow a path through the tree.

In the example regarding purchases from a supermarket, we could decide that we only wish to consider female purchasers. This would be a user-specified branch, such that only data associated with female purchasers need be considered from the outset. The branch (section of the total data set) dealing with male purchasers can be completely ignored by the AI system.

However, we may also input other requirements, the resultant branches of which could be discovered as a part of the analysis. For example, only those purchasers who spend more than £60 per visit, regularly purchase soup and buy fresh vegetables. Rather than dealing with a large number of people (say 50,000), we may, with such a small subset generated by the specific criteria, only need to consider 1,000 or even less, which will dramatically reduce the time taken for the analysis, and at the same time will improve the accuracy of the results and subsequently any predictions made.

FUZZY TREES

I've already described the tree as a logical decision routine to chop up the entire database. This need not be the case as we can have **fuzzy trees**. In the example I mentioned 'regularly' in terms of the frequency of purchasing soup. We could define 'regularly' in a straightforward (logical) way, e.g. at least once per month is regular, less than that (on average) is not. Conversely, we could define 'regularly' in a fuzzy way, e.g. never is 0% and every week is 100%, and any frequency in between these values is fuzzified with an associated percentage – so an individual who purchases soup once every two months might be associated with a fuzzy value of 26% (for example).

Fuzzifying the decision tree in this way still reduces the complexity of the analysis in terms of the number of different parameters (food products in this case) considered. However, any final results will have a level of confidence associated with them. Someone who scores 26% on soup purchasing will not be as strong a member of the final group as someone who scores 84%.

Similar fuzzifying can be carried out in terms of other quantities. In our example one person could spend £10 per week on fresh vegetables while another might spend £25 per week on the same produce. Both individuals could purchase fresh vegetables every week, but clearly we might be more interested in one shopper than the other. We may wish to put more emphasis on the high-spending shopper, especially when it comes to making a prediction.

One option is to increase the dimensions of the database by simply recording more separate values. This is not such a good idea as, in these circumstances, at any one time, an entry will appear in only one of the new split sections (e.g. high spender on vegetables *or* low spender on vegetables). More appropriate is the fuzzy concept of assigning a percentage value to the person with regard to the amount spent. This quantity can then be linked with the frequency of purchase to provide an overall percentage value for an individual. So, an individual may be given a total membership value of (say) 47% in the vegetable-purchasing database because they spend £18 on vegetables, but only buy them once per fortnight.

APPLICATIONS

As we have seen, data mining is very useful for marketing products as it is possible to analyse purchasing patterns and behaviour and then to target any offers to a specific group of people in a way appropriate for that group. Data mining is also useful for analysing business movements and finance, such as the stock market. Trends can be predicted and potential outcomes can be estimated if certain deals are carried out.

One relatively new area for data mining to be used is in detecting criminal activity. First, typical behaviours of groups of people, and even of certain individuals, can be accurately monitored and then any deviations can be quickly highlighted as the activity will not correlate well with previous behaviour. In this way crimes such as fraud can be identified or usage of a stolen credit card can be flagged.

CONCLUDING REMARKS

The classical AI techniques described here have been based more on trying to get machines/computers to copy humans in tasks that, when humans do those tasks, we deem them to be intelligent acts. The discussion has ranged from the ways we store information, as described in the frame technique, to the ways we reason and make decisions, as considered in rule-based expert systems. After all, such an expert system is merely trying to mimic how an expert deals with certain problems.

A motivation for such developments has been evidenced by some of the advantages of AI when compared with human intelligence, which gives us a practical reason to use machines in this context – to replace humans! These include speed of processing, accuracy of mathematical calculations, extent of memory, relating complex data and the ability to function 24 hours per day, seven days per week. Clearly, computers think in a different way to humans!

The concept of intelligence is in itself a controversial topic, but when we consider machines as being intelligent this raises enormous debate. What does this mean? How does machine intelligence compare with human intelligence? Can a machine actually be alive? In the next chapter we look at the important philosophical issues that underpin the subject area.

KEY TERMS

best first search, bucket brigade, common sense knowledge, frames, fuzzy trees, greedy best first search, hill climbing, local search, steepest descent

FURTHER READING

1   *Essence of Artificial Intelligence* by A. Cawsey, published by Prentice-Hall, 2007. This popular book is billed as 'a concise and accessible introduction to the topic for students with no prior knowledge of AI'. It actually deals mainly with very classical AI. It does use case studies very well though, and seems to be quite a neat book in terms of depth. It is written in plain, easy to understand English with abbreviations and technical jargon being fully explained: no knowledge of a programming language is assumed.

2   *Introduction to Artificial Intelligence* by P. Jackson, published by Dover, 1986. This is typical of a number of books on AI. Quite heavy, very classical, dealing mainly with programming languages and with little to do with intelligence. If programming is what you want then this is a useful resource, but if you are interested in AI then books of this type are to be avoided.

3   *Artificial Intelligence: A Modern Approach* by S. Russell and P. Norvig, published by Prentice Hall, 2009. A very good, comprehensive book on classical AI – strongly recommended in that context. Despite the title, it does not deal well with modern AI; indeed, much of the content of the last three chapters of this book is not considered.

4   *Artificial Intelligence: A Systems Approach* by M.T. Jones, published by Jones and Bartlett, 2008. This book is good for programmers who want to realise practical, classical AI systems.

5   *Artificial Intelligence* by P.H. Winston, published by Addison-Wesley, 1992. A classical book on classical AI. A little dated now, but nicely written and introduces ideas in a smooth way. It was a best seller on the subject.

3

THE PHILOSOPHY OF AI

SYNOPSIS

The philosophy behind AI has played a critical role in the subject's development. What does it mean for a machine to think? Can a machine be conscious? Can a machine fool you, in conversation, into thinking it is human? If so, is this important? This whole topic emphasises the importance of the subject by asking fundamental questions about ourselves. We look in this chapter specifically at the Turing Test, the Chinese room problem and conscious machines.

INTRODUCTION

The most important issue when considering arguments about intelligence, whether it is of the human, animal or artificial kind is what exactly intelligence is in the first place. This is something that we looked at in Chapter 1, and in doing so attempted to consider intelligence in a general sense rather than simply the human version.

Unfortunately, as we will see through a number of key examples, the philosophical study of AI has been dogged by the desire to regard human intelligence as something special, and simply to try and show how computers can't do some of the things that human brains do, and therefore the conclusion has been drawn that computers are somehow inferior. This is probably understandable — after all, we are human and it is easy to fall into the trap of thinking that the human way of doing things is the best way.

It is extremely difficult to be objective about something when you are immersed in it on a daily basis. Ask any company whose product is best and, naturally, they will tell you it is theirs. Ask any academic researcher whose research programme is the most important and deserves to be funded and they will tell you it is theirs. In order to get around this, external assessment is required.

Many magazines on the high street are sold simply because in their pages one can read about comparisons between products such as vehicles or washing machines. We respect the magazines' authors as knowledgeable, independent sources who will give us an unbiased view on all the aspects of the products we are interested in. We can then make up our own minds on which product is best (in some way) by analysing all the facts.

In a sense we do this in a scientific way – balancing price with performance with reliability and so on. In doing so, perhaps some aspects are more important to one person than they are to another.

In order to study the philosophy of AI we need to start by carrying out an independent assessment of intelligence. We need, for a moment, to try to forget that we are human and to look at human intelligence from the outside. Perhaps it might be easiest to imagine that you are an alien from another planet, with no preconceived bias towards humans, and you must assess the intelligence of the entities that you observe on Earth.

STARTING POINT

First, let's have a look at some of the misconceptions and biases that can occur and some important points to draw. With AI we are, as we will see, not necessarily trying to copy (simulate) the workings of the human brain. Nevertheless, one interesting initial question might be: could we simulate/copy the human brain with an AI brain?

One approach might be to take human brain cells and to grow them in a laboratory and, when they are connected and developed, put them in a body. This would, we assume, come pretty close to being a human brain. But even then, would it be exactly the same as a human brain if it was in a robot or animal body? It would not have experienced life as a human, with the range of experiences and education. But then, not all humans have a wide range of experiences and there are considerable differences in performance between different human brains. We will look at this particular type of AI, in a practical sense, in Chapter 5.

However, if we take a computer form of AI, which historically has been that most widely considered, then, as John Searle stated, 'a computer simulation of a physical process (e.g. a human brain) is a very different thing from the actual process itself'. Unless we build the brain of exactly the same material, we will never get it to be exactly the same, although, in theory, we might get very close.

With a computer-based AI there will, as a result, always be, the argument goes, some differences between it and a human brain. It is worth remembering, though, that human brains are diverse in their nature and performance – we need to include in our analysis humans who have autism, Alzheimer's disease, cerebral palsy and so on. It must also be remembered, for example, that some humans have a limited or even no form of communication with other humans – however, they are still humans.

PENROSE'S PITFALL

We can all fall into simple traps when studying AI and the human brain. As an example, consider random behaviour. It might be said that computers think in a mechanistic, programmed way, whereas humans can think randomly. This is incorrect – all human thoughts are from and in our brains and are therefore based on the genetic make-up of our brains and what we have learnt in our lives. While an act may appear random to an outside observer, this is simply because they do not understand the reasoning behind it. Anything you do or say will have been based on the signals in your brain. As a simple test, do something random, say something at random. Whatever your action or utterance, *you* will have made a decision to make that specific response.

Roger Penrose, a mathematical physicist, said: 'There is a great deal of randomness in the (human) brain's wiring.' This is simply not true. A human brain is certainly an extremely complex network of highly connected brain cells, but the connections have been made due to biological growth, partly as directed by our genetic make-up and partly down to learning experiences, which physically change the strengths of the connections.

Just because something is complex and difficult to understand does not mean it is random. For example, if you do not understand what is going on, the functioning of a telephone exchange can appear complex to an observer – but it does not act randomly, otherwise we would almost never be able to make a telephone call, we could be connected with absolutely anyone else (at random).

Let us take another argument from Roger Penrose, which is laced with human bias and a desire for humans in general to have something extra. By comparing merely humans and computers we will first look at Penrose's argument – see if you agree with it! We start by considering some form of communication and/or instructions:

1 'Genuine intelligence requires that genuine understanding must be present' or quite simply 'intelligence requires understanding'. In other words, if you don't understand things then you cannot be intelligent.
2 'Actual understanding could not be achieved by any computer.' Put another way, computers will never be able to understand.
3 As a result: 'Computers would always remain subservient to us [humans], no matter how far they advance.'

The general argument of points 1 and 2 appears to be that humans *understand* things, whether it be communication or an inspection of the world around us, and that this is the critical element necessary for intelligence. The argument continues that computers may indeed be able to do things, such as communicate, but they do not *understand* what they are doing, so they cannot be intelligent. Point 3 then follows with the conclusion that computers will always be subservient to humans, on the basis that human intelligence is superior to AI, because AI will never be able to reach the human standard of understanding.

To counter the argument let us broaden the discussion to intelligence in general, including animals. Many creatures appear to communicate or give instruction to each other: we can readily observe this in creatures such as cows, bees and ants, as well as chimpanzees, bats and so on. When one bat screeches to another or when one cow moos to another they presumably have some concept of what is being uttered; indeed, they often seem to respond and interact with each other. One bat appears to understand another bat; one cow appears to understand another cow. But do we humans understand them, can we communicate with them? No.

Using the same arguments put forward by Penrose – as humans do not genuinely understand bats, cows, etc., we are not as intelligent as they are. As a result we will always be subservient to them – bats or cows will rule the Earth! Clearly, such an argument is silly – as, in exactly the same way, is Penrose's argument for computers always being subservient to humans.

Computers may well understand things in a different way to humans; animals probably understand things in different ways to humans; some humans probably understand some things in different ways to other humans. This doesn't make one intelligent and another not. It merely means that one is intelligent in a different way to another. It's all subjective, as was pointed out in Chapter 1.

As for Penrose's third point. Well, that is pure Hollywood, total fiction. It may make someone feel nice to *say* that machines will always be subservient to humans, but there is no logic to it at all. When the Aztecs and the Native Americans were defeated by Europeans it could be said that the 'better', more intelligent culture lay with the home teams. What the invaders brought with them though, apart from disease, was a vastly superior technology that the home teams didn't understand and never got to grips with. We must conclude that just because something is not intelligent in the same way as we humans are does not mean it will always be subservient to us!

WEAK AI

There exist different schools of thought as to the actual nature of AI. These differing philosophical ideals are generally split into three camps, although there may be some overlap.

The possibility that machines can act intelligently as a human does or act as if they were as intelligent as a human is referred to as **weak AI**. This concept stems from Marvin Minsky's definition of AI cited in Chapter 1, whereby machines do things that appear to be intelligent acts. This concept of weak AI is not accepted by some, however.

Computers can, in fact, even now do many things better than (all) humans do, including things that we feel require understanding – playing chess, for example. Humans use computers on a daily basis because of their memory and mathematical abilities, because they can perform in a better way than humans in many aspects of these fields.

STRONG AI

The possibility that a machine can actually think in exactly the same way as a human, as opposed simply to appearing to simulate human thinking, is referred to as **strong AI**. For this to hold, it would mean that it would be possible to build a computer that completely replicated the functioning of the human brain in every aspect.

There are a number of important issues here if it is to be possible for a machine to think in exactly the same way as a human. In particular, a computer will most likely not have had life's rich experiences, as a human would have done, over many years. It would not have grown up experiencing different sensations, realising different values, being faced with moral dilemmas. It may well not have been treated in the same way as a human has. Perhaps most important of all, the computer's body, if it has one (possibly in a robot form), may well be completely different to a human body. It could have wheels rather than legs and an infrared sensor rather than eyes.

A major issue, therefore, with the concept of strong AI is the mind–body problem and the concept of **consciousness**, with associated questions relating to understanding, as we have been discussing, and awareness. Perhaps the best argument brought to bear here is the **brain-in-a-vat experiment**. Imagine there are two versions of your brain. Version 1 is the normal version, the one you are used to. Version 2 can be considered as discussed in the following section.

BRAIN-IN-A-VAT EXPERIMENT

When you are born your brain is removed and placed in a vat, where it is kept alive and fed with suitable nutrients to allow it to grow and develop connections. Electro-chemical signals are sent to the brain over this period to feed it with a purely fictional world, and motor signals from the brain are sent to the world such that you (your brain) are able to modify it and, apparently, move around in it. The *Matrix*-like world appears to you to be real. In theory, your brain, in this state, could have the same sort of feelings and emotions as a brain which has developed in a body in the usual way.

Assuming that the two versions of brain in this discussion have been physically able to develop in identical ways (same temperature, same knocks, same stimulation, etc.) then it all rests on the nature of the fictional world. If it was absolutely identical to the real world then there would be no way to tell the difference and the brains must have developed in exactly the same way. In practice, however, all simulations are not quite the same as the real thing and therefore there would be, in reality, very small discrepancies – referred to as 'qualia', intrinsic experiences.

A supporter of the strong AI argument would believe that any differences between the two versions of your brain are so slight as not to matter; however, an opponent of the argument would feel that no matter how small they are, such differences are absolutely critical.

Underpinning this philosophical discussion is the standpoint that each individual takes. There are those who approach the subject from a materialist viewpoint, assuming that there are no spiritual aspects involved, there is no such thing as the immortal soul, and that 'brains cause minds'. Conversely, there are those who believe that no matter what physical elements are involved, where the (human) brain is concerned, there is something else that cannot be measured and it is this that is the important thing.

From a scientific basis, the first case is the more obvious. There may be some very small differences, but the brain in the simulation could be near enough the same as the actual brain.

In the second case it can be pointless to argue with someone who says that no matter what we witness, no matter what we can experience or measure, there is something else – possibly God-like – at work and that overrides all else. This is not a scientific approach.

As a result there are two closely related topics which come up for discussion. The first of these is the concept of **free will**. How can a mind, restricted by physical constructs, achieve freedom of choice? One purely materialistic argument to this swiftly concludes that free will is merely the decisions taken by an individual – and that these are based on their genetic make-up, their experience and the sensed environment at that time.

The other, more widely discussed topic is the general issue of the deeper operation of the inner functioning of the brain: *consciousness*, with related questions of understanding and self-awareness. Example questions can be posed, such as: what does it *feel* like to smell a rose? This can be followed up with: how can a computer possibly *feel* such a thing? Further points can be made, such as: why does it *feel* like something to have brain states whereas presumably it does not *feel* like anything to be a shoe? As a result, conclusions can then be drawn that a shoe (and hence a computer) cannot be conscious!

Issues raised regarding consciousness are often liberally laced with human-centric bias which, to view the subject scientifically, we need to overcome. First, as a human we *know* what it is like to be ourselves. We do not *know* what it is like to be anything else, such as a bat, a computer, another human, a cabbage, a rock or a shoe. We should not therefore *presume* we know what someone or something else is thinking. We certainly should not conclude that because something else is not the same as us, therefore it doesn't think in as good a way as us or even that it cannot think at all.

Second, the arguments considered often apply human bias to the nature of any effect being felt. What is required to 'smell' a rose is the human sense of smell. Smelling a rose is something of value to a human; it may or may not be of value to a dog. A shoe, from scientific analysis thus far, does not appear to have a sense of smell.

Third, a (presumably normal) human is (in the argument) compared with a shoe, with a supposed follow-on assumption that a computer is similar to a shoe, allowing the conclusion to be drawn regarding the consciousness of a shoe to also apply to a computer. The argument states: if a shoe is not conscious then a computer cannot be conscious! I have to say that I have not yet witnessed a shoe that is similar to a computer.

Comparing a human with a shoe in this way and likening the shoe to a computer is akin to comparing a computer with a cabbage and then likening the cabbage to a human. Can the cabbage deal with mathematics, communicate in English or control a jet aircraft?

Exactly the same logic as used in the shoe–computer consciousness argument for humans would mean that if a cabbage can't do these things then neither can a human. Clearly these are ridiculous comparisons, but so too is comparing a human with a shoe, or other such inanimate object, in this way.

RATIONAL AI

The possibility that a machine can act as if it was as intelligent as a human is referred to as weak AI, whereas the possibility that a machine can actually think in exactly the same way as a human is referred to as strong AI. Both of these positions suffer from the fact that a human-centric comparison is going on, to the extent that a starting point is taken that there is only one intelligence – human intelligence – to which all other forms of intelligence (including presumably that of aliens if they exist!) must aspire.

In fact, the distinction drawn here appears to have been proposed back in the early days of AI, when computers merely operated on symbols. Clear links could then be shown between the embodied biological form of intelligence of humans and the disembodied **symbolic processing** of computers, no matter how fast and accurate those computers might have been.

What is needed now is an up-to-date viewpoint that is not only representative of the computers, machines and robots of today, but that also encapsulates the different forms of intelligence witnessed in life in its broadest sense. A modern, open view of consciousness, understanding, self-awareness and free will is required for us to really get to terms with modern AI.

As a start, assume for a moment that an alien being lands on Earth, having travelled billions of miles from its own planet in order to do so. Most likely it will have intellectual properties way beyond those of humans as humans have not yet figured out how to travel as far in the opposite direction and stay alive. But if the alien is of a completely different form to humans – maybe the alien is a machine – then would we say that it is not aware of itself because it is not like me, a human? Would we say it is not conscious because it does not think in exactly the same way as we do? It is doubtful that the alien would bother too much about our idle thoughts. Yet the alien may well not come up to scratch against our definition of weak AI, never mind in terms of strong AI.

We need a viewpoint on AI that is much less anthropomorphic than the classical AI considered thus far. We need to include features such as distributed information processing, agent autonomy, embeddedness, sensory motor coupling with the environment, various forms of social interaction and more. In each case humans exhibit such features but so too do other animals and some machines.

We need to incorporate psychological and cognitive characteristics, such as memory, without which it is unlikely that a truly intelligent behaviour can be observed. We also need to be open to the fact that any behaviour that can be characterised in this way is truly intelligent regardless of the nature of the being that generated it.

Rational AI means that any artefact fulfilling such a general definition can act intelligently and think in its own right, in its own way. Whether this turns out to be in any sense similar to the intelligence, thought, consciousness, self-awareness, etc. of a human is neither here nor there. Concepts such as weak AI and strong AI therefore retain their meaning in the limited sense in which they have been generated, i.e. with regard to the human form of intelligence.

In the same way, other creatures conforming to such a rational definition of AI are intelligent and think in their own way, dependent on their particular senses and how their brain is structured.

AI, in the sense of machines, whether they be of silicon or carbon forms, then takes its place as one version of intelligence, different in some ways, appearance and characteristics from human and animal intelligence. Indeed, just as humans are intelligent in different ways from each other, so AI is diverse in itself in terms of the different types of machines that are apparent.

BRAIN PROSTHESIS EXPERIMENT

Quite a number of interesting philosophical arguments using AI as a basis have arisen and no book on AI would be complete without taking a look at some of them. The first of these is the brain prosthesis experiment. For this argument we must presume that scientific understanding has progressed to such an extent that we can fully understand the working of human brain cells (neurons) and can perfectly engineer microscopic devices which perform exactly the same function.

Surgical techniques have, the argument continues, developed at an equally astounding pace to the extent that it is possible to replace individual neurons in a human brain with their microscopic equivalents without interrupting the workings of the brain as a whole. Cell by cell the whole brain is replaced. Once complete it is then gradually restored to its original self by reversing the process again cell by cell.

So the question is, for the individual involved, would their consciousness remain the same throughout the whole process? Some philosophers argue one way and some the other.

If the individual smells a flower when in both versions, either:

1 consciousness that generates the resultant feelings still operates in the technological version, which is therefore conscious in the same way as the original; or
2 conscious mental events in the original brain have no connection to behaviour and are therefore missing in the technological version, which as a result is not conscious.

Presumably, once the reversal occurs the individual will be conscious although they may or may not suffer memory loss in the meantime.

Version 2 is what is called **epiphenomenal**, something which occurs but which has no effect whatsoever in the real world. This has little/no scientific basis at all. It is a case of no matter what results are obtained and no matter how much the technological brain is an exact copy of the original, the human original simply must have something extra, even if we cannot measure it and cannot witness any action which results from it.

Version 1 requires that the replacement neurons, and their connections, are identical to the original. If we assume that we can, using present-day physics, completely and accurately form a mathematical model of the human brain (which actually appears not to be possible at the present time) then surely, in time, we would be able to carry out the experiment in this way.

One argument against version 1 says that although we might be able to copy the neurons extremely closely, we would *never* be able to copy them exactly. It goes on that subtle differences due to chaotic behaviour or quantum randomness would still exist and it is these differences that are critical. Note: an older argument along the same lines (that you might come across) also suggested that it was the continuous nature of the human brain as opposed to the digital nature of a computer that was critical. The advent of the type of AI based on grown biological brains, as discussed in Chapter 5, has put paid to that argument.

Another more plausible argument, by Roger Penrose, says that it is our present-day understanding of physics that is to blame. He feels that for the very small elements that cannot be copied 'such non-computational action would have to be found in an area of physics that lies outside the presently known physical laws'. He goes on to suggest that if we could discover these laws then version 1 would be quite possible.

In the brain prosthesis argument we are not concerned as to whether or not the technological brain is conscious, but whether or not it is conscious in the same way as the original human brain. In the previous discussion of rational AI, the possibility of AI to be conscious, in its own way, is not in question. What is in question here is whether this could be identical to human consciousness.

As a reality check, a number of issues need to be raised: first, as pointed out earlier, no matter how good the technological neuron models, there will in practical terms be differences between the human and technological brain unless the replacement neurons happen to actually be the same human neurons that were removed in the first place. On the other hand, the model could be very close, which means that the form of consciousness exhibited by the technological brain could be extremely close to that of the original human brain, to the degree that (in an engineering sense) it makes no difference.

A further point, however, is that this is a purely philosophical exercise. The human brain is an extremely complex organ, full of highly connected neurons. If even just one neuron is removed through surgery then the overall effect may be negligible, but it *can* be dramatic, with the individual's behaviour changing completely.

As an example: such dramatic changes can be readily witnessed in the human brain as a result of deep brain stimulation treatment for Parkinson's disease.

THE CHINESE ROOM PROBLEM

The Chinese room is the scene for an argument originated by John Searle in an attempt to show that a symbol-processing machine (a computer) can never be properly described as *having a mind* or *understanding* or *being conscious*, no matter how intelligently it may behave. It has become a cornerstone argument in the philosophy of AI, with researchers either supporting his case or attempting to provide counter arguments. Let us start by considering the argument itself.

A computer (inside a room) takes Chinese characters as input and follows the instructions of a program to produce other Chinese characters, which it presents as output.

The computer does this so convincingly that it comfortably convinces an external human Chinese speaker that it is itself a human Chinese speaker – effectively it passes the Turing Test (discussed in a later section), it fools another human into believing that it is, itself, human.

It could be argued by a supporter of strong AI that the computer *understands* Chinese. However, Searle argues that if the machine doesn't have *understanding* we cannot describe what the machine is doing as *thinking*. If this is the case then because it does not think, it does not have a *mind* in anything like the normal sense of the word. Therefore, 'strong AI' is mistaken.

Consider that you are in a closed room and that you (an English speaker who understands no Chinese) have a rule book with an English version of the same program. You can receive Chinese characters, process them according to the instructions, and as a result you produce Chinese characters as output. As the computer has convinced a human Chinese speaker that it is itself a Chinese speaker it is fair to deduce that you will be able to do so as well.

There is in essence no difference between the computer's role in the first case and the role you play in the latter. Each is simply following a program which simulates intelligent behaviour. Yet (as we have presumed) you do not understand a word of Chinese, you are merely following instructions. Since you do not understand Chinese we can infer that the computer does not understand Chinese either – as both you and the computer perform exactly the same function. The conclusion drawn by Searle is therefore that running a computer program does not generate understanding.

THE EMERGENCE OF CONSCIOUSNESS

Searle's argument is essentially that you (a human) have something more than the machine; you have a mind which could learn to understand Chinese and that your mind is realised through the type of brain that you have. Searle said: 'The [human] brain is an organ. Consciousness [and understanding] is caused by lower-level neuronal processes in the brain and is itself a feature of the brain. It is an emergent property of the brain.' He continued: 'Consciousness is not a property of any individual elements and it cannot be explained simply as a summation of the properties of those elements.' He concluded: 'Computers are useful devices for simulating brain processes. But the simulation of mental states is no more a mental state than the simulation of an explosion is itself an explosion.'

The very last line (Searle's conclusion) here is importantly and appropriately refuting the concept of strong AI – much as was discussed earlier. However, in the argument made, Searle opens up a number of other important considerations.

First is the concept that you (a human) have something extra that the computer does not have (consciousness) and that this comes about as an emergent property of your brain – through your human neurons and their connections! This could be seen as epiphenomenal, in that there are 'properties' in human neurons that give rise to the mind, but these properties cannot be detected by anyone outside the mind, otherwise they could possibly be simulated in a computer, thus realising strong AI. These extra differences in the human brain are perhaps the qualia referred to by Penrose.

One point here is that this is a good example of an argument in AI in which human intelligence is seen to be something special. It appears that even if we can't measure it, the human brain is deemed to have something more than a machine brain. The argument is human-centric. It is concerned with a human language, with all the nuances and life experiences that that conjures up. Without having lived a human life, could a machine possibly *understand* such a language in the same way as a human? This is indeed Searle's point – no matter how much the computer is used in an attempt to copy the human brain, it will never be exactly the same – unless perhaps it is itself made up of human neurons and experiences some aspects of human life.

The Chinese room argument can be refuted in a number of ways. As an example, the argument can be turned on its head and posed in a favourable way for a machine by considering a machine code communication – with exactly the same type of argument. You now have to follow a set of instructions with regard to machine code rather than Chinese. On the basis that no matter what you might learn, the machine code will still mean nothing to you, you will not *understand* it, whereas, for all we know, a computer may well *understand* the machine code. The end conclusion of such an argument would be that while a machine can be conscious, it is not possible for a human to be conscious.

Searle has used his Chinese room argument in a number of different ways. He has said that while 'humans have beliefs, thermostats and adding machines do not' or (as discussed earlier) 'if a shoe is not conscious then how can a computer be conscious?'. As indicated earlier, the exact same logic would argue that if a cabbage is not conscious then how can a human be conscious?

Perhaps the most important aspect of human understanding and consciousness to conclude from this is that they are likely (as Searle postulated) emergent properties from the collective behaviour of human neurons. We will investigate this further, with intriguing consequences, in Chapter 5.

TECHNOLOGICAL SINGULARITY

One of the interesting and vitally important features to be gleaned from the study of machine intelligence is its potential not simply to be the same as, but to surpass human intelligence at some stage. The argument goes that it is intelligence that has put humans in their relatively powerful position on Earth and if something comes along that is more intelligent then this could pose a threat to human dominance. Already, computers outperform humans in a number of ways – aspects of mathematics, memory, sensory faculties, etc. Perhaps it is just a matter of time before a superintelligent machine appears, which can then design and produce even more superintelligent machines and so on.

Such a situation, where humans could lose control, was referred to as the 'technological singularity' by Vinge in 1993. He said: 'Within 30 years we will have the technological means to create superhuman intelligence.' Moravec contributed: 'Robots will match human intelligence in 50 years then exceed it – they will become our Mind Children.'

Because of this potential threat some people interestingly turn (for safety?) to the **three laws of robotics**, introduced by the science fiction writer Isaac Asimov, as though they have some scientific basis. The laws are:

1   A robot may not injure a human being or through inaction allow a human being to come to harm.
2   A robot must obey the orders given by a human unless this conflicts with law 1.
3   A robot must protect its own existence unless this conflicts with laws 1 or 2.

Although these laws are purely fictional they have been taken by some as though they are strict regulations to which robots must adhere. Let us be clear – they are simply fictional ideas, nothing more, nothing less. Further, it is not apparent that any real-world robot has ever operated under these rules. Indeed, if we consider many military robotic machines of today, they blatantly break all three of the laws in their everyday use.

Because of the potential loss of control by humans to machines, as a means perhaps to combat such an eventuality, various researchers have suggested a merger between humans and technology. Kurzweil predicted 'a strong trend toward the merger of human thinking with the world of machine intelligence', indicating further that 'there will no longer be any clear distinction between humans and computers'.

Steven Hawking poignantly commented:

> In contrast with our intellect, computers double their perform-ance every 18 months. The danger is real that they could develop intelligence and take over the world. We must develop as quickly as possible technologies that make a direct connec-tion between brain and computer.

Research in the area suggested by Hawking has in fact been going on for some time, partly with regard to using such technology to assist those humans with a disability of one type or another. However, the area of human enhancement has also sprung up, investigating new sensory input and new means of communication for humans. The age of the cyborg – part human, part machine – has commenced.

THE TURING TEST

Arguably the most contentious and certainly the best known philo-sophical discussion relating to AI is what has become known as the Turing Test. In fact, it was originally proposed by Alan Turing in 1950 as an imitation game. His intention was to look at the ques-tion of 'Can a machine think?' or, indeed, 'Is a machine intelli-gent?' in the same way as we might consider whether or not another human can think or is intelligent.

If we wished to test another human with regard to their intelli-gence, we might ask them questions or discuss topics with them, drawing our conclusions on this basis – much as is normally done in a standard job interview. So maybe we could do the same sort of thing with a machine!

When considering the intelligence of a computer, rather than listing a whole string of features characteristic of intelligence, many of which would be controversial and some irrelevant, what Turing pro-posed was to test a machine as to its indistinguishability from humans, the idea being that if you converse with a computer for a period and can't tell the difference between it and a human, then you must credit it with the same sort of intelligence as you would credit a human.

The test in its basic form is as follows. An interrogator faces a keyboard attached to a split computer monitor. Behind one half of the screen is a computer respondent, behind the other is a human respondent. Both the human and computer respondents are hidden from view, possibly in another room, and the only interaction allowable is communication via the keyboard and monitor. The interrogator has five minutes to discuss whatever he/she likes with the two unknown entities. At the end of that period the interrogator must decide which hidden entity is the human and which is the computer. The goal of the computer is to fool the interrogator, not that they are human but that they are more human than the hidden human.

In 1950 Turing said:

> I believe that in about fifty years' time it will be possible to pro-gramme computers … to make them play the imitation game so well that an average interrogator will not have more than 70% chance of making the right identification after five minutes of questioning.

This is what has become known as the Turing Test.

The wording Turing used was a little confusing. What it means is that to pass the Turing Test a computer needs to fool an average interrogator into making an incorrect decision at least 30% of the time.

In the computer's favour is the fact that the computer does not actually have to fool the interrogator that it is human and that the hidden human is a machine, although that is the best result for the computer. Rather, to score in the computer's favour it is sufficient for the interrogator to be unsure which is which or to think both hidden entities are the same, either human or machine – as these would also be incorrect decisions.

But looked at another way, it is actually a very tough task for the computer. Consider, for example, that instead of a machine and a human sitting behind the monitor, we have two humans, both trying to get the interrogator to believe that they are human but that the other entity is a computer. Effectively, the interrogator would choose which entity of the two he/she thought was most human-like. Achieving a score of 50% for one of the humans would be expected from average scoring; however, anything higher would mean that the other human has scored less than 50%.

Clearly it is quite possible (in fact very likely) for a reasonably intelligent human, pitted against another human, to fail the Turing Test by scoring less than 30%. Looked at in this way the Turing Test is quite a challenge in that a computer must fool interrogators that it is more human than many humans.

The test is normally expected to be conducted in English, although any language would prove the point. But what about the hidden humans taking part? Are they adults, children, native English speakers, experts, do they have illnesses (e.g. dementia), do they try to be human or machine? Turing did not stipulate the exact nature of these hidden humans, which poses interesting questions in itself as to who (what sort of humans) the computer is competing against.

Another problem area with the test (in terms of practically carrying out such a study) is the concept of an **average interrogator**. In any actual practical tests that occur it is invariably interested parties who are involved as interrogators. These include professors of computer science, philosophers, journalists and even students of AI – none of which, in the circumstances, can be considered *average*.

To obtain a true statistical 'average' an extremely large number of interrogators would need to include some people who cannot use a computer, some who are not able to understand what they are supposed to do, some non-native language interrogators, some very young children, people from all different walks of life and so on. In terms of actual results this would most likely help towards the computer's apparent performance, as any uncertainty or inability to make the 'right identification' helps the computer's cause.

WHAT DOES THE TURING TEST ACTUALLY TEST?

Turing posed the game instead of answering the question 'Can machines think?'. The test/game indicates that a machine 'appears' to think in the same way as a human (if it passes)! We might ask, though, could we do any better if we tested a human – how do we know that they think?

The test does not, however, deal with issues such as consciousness or self-awareness, other than can be gleaned through questioning. The nature of the interrogation carried out is therefore an important factor.

Turing himself said 'Intelligent behaviour presumably consists in a departure from the completely disciplined behaviour involved in computation, but rather a slight one, which does not give rise to random behaviour, or to pointless repetitive loops.' It is therefore down to a Turing Test interrogator to bring such aspects into play during a conversation.

At the time of this book going to press, no computer has officially passed the Turing Test. So what about Turing's conjecture that by the year 2000, it would be possible for a computer to be programmed to pass his test? It is interesting to consider what Turing actually said. First (in 1950), he said in 'about' 50 years' time, not 'exactly'; and second, he said that it would be possible to programme computers to pass the test – not that necessarily a computer would have passed the test by 2000. It is very useful, however, to take a look at where things stand now.

LOEBNER COMPETITION

Occasionally an 'official' Turing Test is carried out under strict rules, to assess the state of play. Every year, however, an open competition sponsored by Hugh Loebner is held, following some of Turing's stipulations. Although usually it is not exactly as directed by Turing himself, it does give us some idea of where things stand. Most important of all, it gives an intriguing insight into conversational features of the interrogators, the machines and even the hidden humans.

Each year the Loebner competition is aimed at finding the best conversational machine from those that are entered. The format of the event is that parallel-paired comparisons (as just described – one human/one machine) are made between each of four hidden machines pitted in turn against each of four hidden humans in a 25-minute test. The task of each interrogator is to identify the machine and human in each test pair, assigning a total mark out of 100 to the pair (so a mark of Entry A 49/Entry B 51 would mean that in that particular paired interrogation entry B is deemed to be very slightly more human than A, whereas a mark of Entry A 94/Entry B 6 would mean the interrogator believes that entry A is almost certainly the human and entry B the machine).

It might be expected that over time as AI and machine technology improve so the top score achieved by a machine in the annual Loebner competition will generally improve year on year. Yet in the 2001 competition, one machine was deemed by two out of the five interrogators to be more human than any of the hidden humans present. However, in the same competition in 2006, no machine was deemed to be more human than any of the hidden humans. In fact, over the three-year period 2004–2006 the highest score obtained by any machine from any one of the interrogators was: 2004 = 48; 2005 = 45; 2006 = 28.

It is not easy to pinpoint the reasons for this. Perhaps the expectations of Loebner judges/interrogators are increasing as they gain in knowledge of how to trick the machines, or could it be that the machines themselves are getting worse? On top of this, no machine from 2003 to 2007 deceived any interrogator that it was human, whereas this was a regular occurrence prior to 2003.

One reason appears to be that Hugh Loebner has insisted that each test lasts for 25 minutes, as opposed to Turing's stipulation of five minutes. Another major factor is that networking (a big advantage of AI) has been disallowed due to the possibility of a linked-in human pretending to be a machine pretending to be a human in order to win the prize money offered by Hugh Loebner!

CAN A MACHINE TELL A JOKE?

How can a machine be caught out in conversation? For example, could humour catch the machine out? Surely, you might argue, a machine cannot have a sense of humour. One philosopher (Rickman) asserted in 1999 that 'computers, whatever artificial intelligence they may display, cannot make jokes'. If he is right then this would be an easy give away. Could it be possible for a machine to 'create' (produce from its linguistic armoury) an original response that the human receiver may deem witty during conversational interaction? A point to ponder on here is that many of the machines which take part actually learn to communicate through numerous discussions with humans.

What about these examples taken from Loebner transcripts? These were actual responses during the competition in conversation with the machine called 'Jabberwacky':

INTERROGATOR: Ok, but are you always right?
JABBERWACKY: Sometimes I am left.

INTERROGATOR: How small is small anyhow?
JABBERWACKY: Small.
INTERROGATOR: Yes but exactly how small?
JABBERWACKY: Very small.

INTERROGATOR: So why don't you take over the world?
JABBERWACKY: I wouldn't know what to do with it.... Anyway,
I'm pretty busy already.

These examples have been included to show how such machines can cope surprisingly well with some very human conversation and even perhaps upset a philosopher or two.

TURING 2008

In 2008, in order to assess the state of play, the Loebner competition was held at the University of Reading. Under special circumstances and the agreement of Hugh Loebner, strict Turing Test rules were invoked, so a series of five-minute paired machine/human tests were performed with a variety of interrogators. The winning machine was Fred Roberts' Elbot, which succeeded in fooling 25% of its interrogators (30% is the Turing 'pass mark') into thinking it was human. So possibly the machines are almost there as far as the Turing Test is concerned, but perhaps not quite. Curiously, Elbot openly admits to interrogators, when asked, that it is a robot!

Interrogators who took part in 2008 included software engineers, scientists, philosophers and newspaper journalists – certainly not the 'average interrogator' that Turing spoke of.

Various ploys have been used over the years in an attempt to trip up the machines competing. Asking mathematical questions does not work as the machines are not stupid, they are just as unlikely as a human to attempt to give a mathematical answer. It is perhaps better to ask topical or local questions; for example, to discuss what the weather is like or what colour the walls are painted. The point is not whether a machine gives a 'correct' answer, but if it gives one that a human would.

Perhaps you can see for yourself how good you would be as an interrogator. At the Reading competition, one interrogator asked the same question of a number of hidden entities:

What did you think about the weather this morning?

Three different responses came from a male human, a female human and a machine. Which is which? Keep in mind that the event was held in October 2008 and they all knew it was autumn/fall in England. The responses were:

1 'I do tend to like a nice foggy morning, as it adds a certain mystery.'
2 'Not the best, expecting pirates to come out of the fog.'
3 'The weather is not nice at the moment, unless you like fog.'

So which is which? Find the answer at the end of this chapter.

What follows is part of the conversation for which the machine Ultra Hal was scored 'human' by the interrogator concerned:

INTERROGATOR: Morning.
ULTRA HAL: Good morning judge.
ULTRA HAL: It's eight something, maybe you ate something.
ULTRA HAL: Get it?
INTERROGATOR: Yes.

If an entity was deemed to be a machine, the interrogator was also asked to mark the humanness of their conversation out of 100. What follows is part of the conversation for which a non-native English-speaking female (human) was scored 'machine' by the interrogator and was awarded 40/100 for their humanness – the interrogator was pretty certain that they were a machine:

INTERROGATOR: So let's cut to the point. Are you the human or the computer?
HIDDEN HUMAN: What do you think?
INTERROGATOR: That's just the sort of answer I would expect from a computer.

Here's a successful double bluff from the eventual winner, Elbot, during one of the conversations for which Elbot was adjudged by the interrogator to be an adult male:

INTERROGATOR: Okay, fair enough, I'll stop with the slang. How are you?

ELBOT: Just a moment! I'll start my self-diagnosis algorithm and let you know the results.

INTERROGATOR: Very funny, that's exactly what you'd say if you were a computer, right?

One interesting feature from the 2008 competition is that several times when an interrogator was fooled by a machine into thinking that the machine was human, the interrogator not only did not realise their mistake but even considered that they had done very well in easily selecting which entity was human and which was machine in each case.

One interrogator, a journalist for the *Times* newspaper, subsequently wrote a newspaper article describing how it was simple to detect which were the machines – even though he had been fooled on several occasions. Exactly the same was true of a university philosopher, another of the interrogators, who subsequently wrote in an academic paper that a 'couple of questions and answers were usually sufficient to confirm' which was the machine. The philosopher (and his co-workers) actually achieved a 44% wrong identification rate, well above Turing's 30%!

From the 2008 exercise overall, it is clear that machines are not yet at the level of conversational performance set by Turing. However, the best of them are getting quite close. What a machine will have achieved when it passes Turing's target is difficult to say – other than it will have passed the Turing Test. The game is an interesting exercise as well as being an important milestone in AI. As you can see from the examples and related stories, it also tells us quite a bit more about ourselves.

It could be argued that the test is very tough for any machine to pass. Turing himself said:

The game may be criticised because the odds are weighted too heavily against the machine. If the man were to try and pretend to be the machine he would clearly make a very poor showing. He would be given away at once by slowness and inaccuracy in arithmetic. May not machines carry out something which ought to be described as thinking but which is very different from what a man does? This objection is a very strong one, but at least we can say that if, nevertheless, a machine can be constructed to play the imitation game satisfactorily, we need not be troubled by this objection.

ARGUMENT FROM DISABILITY

It is apparent when comparing humans and machines that computers can now do many things better than humans do – in particular, things we feel require understanding, such as playing chess, mathematics, recalling from an extensive memory and so on.

The 'argument from disability', as Turing called it, is the type of argument put up by humans against the abilities of a machine in a defensive fashion. We know that machines can do many things well; however, this appears to provoke a defensive attitude in some people to conclude that no matter what machines can do, humans still have something more. Indeed, this is the foundation of the Chinese room problem.

As Turing put it, some will say 'a machine can never...' Examples given by Turing are: 'be kind, resourceful, beautiful, friendly, have initiative, have a sense of humor, tell right from wrong, make mistakes, fall in love, enjoy strawberries and cream, etc.'.

In fact, there is no reason that a computer could not do any of these things – indeed, in this chapter we have specifically looked further into one such example: the sense of humour. Whether a computer does them in the same way as a human and whether it 'understands' what it is doing in the same way that a human would and whether or not the act is at all meaningful to the machine are quite different questions.

However, we can't know whether another human 'understands' or 'feels' things in the same way that we do. Another person may say and think that they understand – but do they? How can we be sure?

There are many things that machines can do that humans cannot do – flying being a good example. This doesn't make the machine better than humans at everything, it is just one feature. It would be silly to conclude that humans are already generally inferior to machines because we cannot fly.

So when we point to something that a human can do but that apparently a machine may not be able to do, we need to be sensible about what conclusions we draw from that. Is the task an important, defining issue in some sense? After all, most machines are pretty specific in what they are required to do – we would not necessarily expect an aeroplane to smell a rose or to have a dry sense of humour.

If we were trying to build a machine that was an exact replica of a human (both physically and mentally), then it might be appropriate to criticise a particular feature of the machine as not being quite the same. However, no machine has ever been so designed. So why should anyone expect a machine to do absolutely everything that a human can do, as well as a human can do and then go on to do more?

When we consider the argument from disability, the Chinese room and the Turing Test we need to be clear most of all as to what the comparison is meant to prove. Which machine is being compared with which human? Both machines and humans have many different versions with many different abilities, so can we make generalisations as we might like to? Perhaps most important of all, is the comparison important in some sense? If a machine cannot smell a rose or enjoy a cup of tea will this save humans from an intelligent machine take over?

CONCLUDING REMARKS

In the previous chapter we looked at classical AI in which a top-down approach is taken. In this sense a view is taken of human intelligence, like a psychiatrist's testing, from the outside. Hence the basic rules performed in this way by a human, and the way the brain appears to work are copied, to some extent, by the artificially intelligent computer.

As a result of the classical approach taken, it was a natural step to see how close the computer could come to actually performing in exactly the same way as a human in terms of their intelligence. What sprung up was therefore a human-centric philosophical comparative analysis, as we have seen in this chapter. In some ways computers have been able to outperform humans for many years, whereas in other ways – human communication for example, as witnessed by the Turing Test – computers are perhaps not quite yet able to perform in exactly the same way as humans.

The defensive nature of the philosophy that has arisen from classical AI is significant. The basic argument underpinning much of the philosophy encountered appears to be: 'The computer can do lots of things that a human can do but surely humans have something more!' This something more has been called *consciousness* – an abstract term and therefore something that probably cannot be scientifically proven one way or the other. Unfortunately, as we will see, many of the philosophical arguments that appear to hold water as far as classical AI is concerned come unstuck all too quickly as we move forward to a bottom-up, modern approach to AI.

Alan Turing witnessed this over 60 years ago in his categorisation of the argument from disability: machines can do all sorts of things, but they can't ... (whatever). Despite Turing's insightful observation, much of the classical AI philosophy falls foul of exactly that. As an example, this is exactly the conclusion drawn from the Chinese room problem.

In the next chapter we will look at a number of modern approaches to AI, which can be employed on their own, in combination or, if it provides a desired end result, in combination with one of the classical approaches already considered. So onward into neural networks, evolutionary computing and genetic algorithms!

Did you guess correctly that A was the machine, B the male and C the female?

KEY TERMS

average interrogator, brain-in-a-vat experiment, consciousness, epiphenomenal, free will, strong AI, symbolic processing, three laws of robotics, weak AI

FURTHER READING

1   *Introducing Artificial Intelligence* by H. Brighton and H. Selina, published by Icon Books, 2007. This book is an attempt to cover the general historical and philosophical background of AI. It is

certainly accessible for people not in the field of AI, but is very light on detailed explanation. It mainly concentrates on the philosophical issues with some aspects of language. Not really a book for someone expecting a general overview – particularly not for engineering or science students, more for those approaching from the arts side.

2   *Beyond AI: Creating the Conscience of the Machine* by J. Storrs Hall, published by Prometheus Books, 2007. This book looks at the history of AI and predicts future achievements. It considers what this means for society and the relations between technology and human beings. It is mainly concerned with the ethical and societal impact of AI.

3   *Minds and Computers: An Introduction to the Philosophy of Artificial Intelligence* by M. Carter, published by Edinburgh University Press, 2007. This is an excellent next step in reading into the philosophy of AI – it considers the important philosophical issues in slightly greater depth.

4   *The Age of Spiritual Machines: When Computers Exceed Human Intelligence* by R. Kurzweil, published by Penguin Putnam, 2000. This is one of a number of visionary views on the future of AI and the likely relationship that intelligent machines will have with humans.

5   *Views into the Chinese Room: New Essays on Searle and Artificial Intelligence*, edited by J. Preston and M. Bishop, published by Oxford University Press, 2002. This book consists of collected essays on the specific topic of the Chinese room from all of the top philosophical thinkers in the field. A broad range of ideas are presented.

4

MODERN AI

SYNOPSIS

In recent years the modern approach to AI has focused more on bottom-up techniques – that is, to take some of the basic building blocks of intelligence, put them together and get them to learn and develop over a period of time and see where we are. In this chapter you will be gently introduced to artificial neural networks, genetic algorithms and evolutionary computation. Mathematics can easily play a major role in applying these methods – this is not the case in the presentation here. Rather, the aim is to provide a minimally complex guide to the subject without losing meaning – an in-depth mathematical consideration can follow for those who wish to delve deeper.

INTRODUCTION

In Chapter 2 we saw how, with classical AI, the approach is to look at the workings of a brain from the outside and, as a result of our observations, to attempt to replicate its performance in an AI system. This approach is particularly successful at dealing with well-defined tasks for which a set of clear rules are appropriate, particularly when a lot of such rules need to be processed and acted upon in a relatively short time frame. The machine's advantage in speed of memory recall plays an important role in this.

However, the classical AI technique is not so good when it comes to awareness of a situation and making a rough comparison with previously learnt experiences – something which is an extremely important aspect of intelligence. Indeed, for many creatures it is an everyday feature of intelligence. Experiencing life, finding out what works and what doesn't and then when a new, slightly different situation comes along, dealing with it in as good a way as possible, based on the previous experiences. This problem is much better dealt with by looking at how the brain works in a fundamental way.

The first underpinning concept of modern AI is to consider how a biological brain operates in terms of its basic functioning, how it learns, how it evolves and how it adapts over time. The second point is a need to obtain relatively simple models of the fundamental elements – the building blocks, if you like – of the brain. Third, these building blocks are mimicked by a technological design – possibly a piece of electronic circuitry, possibly a computer program, the aim of which is to simulate the building blocks. The artificial building blocks can then be plugged together and modified in different ways to operate in a brain-like fashion.

It may be that the aim of such a study is to copy the original brain in some way, using an artificial version. However, most likely it will simply be a case of taking inspiration from the biological way of working and using that in the technological design. In doing so, the artificial version will benefit from some of the advantages of the original biological brain – for example, the ability to generalise about a result or quite easily classify an event into one category or another.

Initially we will have a look at the basic components of a biological brain such that we can then consider piecing together models of some of the fundamental elements.

BIOLOGICAL BRAIN

The basic cell in a biological brain, a nerve cell, is referred to as a neuron (sometimes you may see it written as neurone – it's the same thing). In a typical human brain there are about 100 billion of these. Each neuron is very small, typically being 2–30 micrometres in diameter (one-thousandth of the size of a small coin). The neurons are connected together to form an extremely complex network, each neuron having upwards of 10,000 connections.

Different creatures have different numbers of neurons with varying complexities of networks. Slugs and snails can have just a few (9–10 for a sea slug) up to a few hundred. Even in these cases the structure and functioning of such a brain is not simple. The neurons are all a little bit different – although some are very different – from each other, not only in terms of size, but also in terms of the strength of their connections with other neurons and which neurons they are connected to.

As far as human neurons are concerned, those that deal with information as it is captured by human senses (sensory neurons) are specialised in dealing with the signals obtained for sight, sound, etc. Meanwhile, those that are employed to send signals out to move muscles (motor neurons) are specialised to achieve that end. There are also neurons that deal with planning, reasoning and so on. Each neuron has a relatively simple structure, but with many of them acting together in a complex way, a biological brain is a powerful tool indeed.

Each neuron consists of a cell body with a nucleus at its centre. A number of fibres, called dendrites, stimulate the cell body with signals from other neurons, as shown in Figure 4.1. Meanwhile, signals are transmitted from the neuron along an axon, which subsequently branches out and connects to the dendrites of other neurons, at points called synapses.

Ordinarily a neuron will be at a resting state, and will receive stimulating signals in the form of electro-chemical pulses (pulses which are both electrical and chemical in nature) along some of the dendrites from other neurons. Each of the pulses received changes the electrical potential (a voltage) of the cell body – some of the dendrites add to the cell potential signal (these are called excitatory), whereas some subtract from it (these are called inhibitory). If the total signal on the dendrites at any time reaches a particular threshold value then that cell will fire an electro-chemical pulse, referred to as an action potential, onto its axon and hence out to other neurons to help them to fire in turn. Shortly after the neuron has fired in this way it returns to its resting state and waits for the pulses on its dendrites to build up again. If, conversely, the threshold value is not reached, then the neuron will not fire. It is an all-or-nothing process – the neuron either fires or it doesn't.

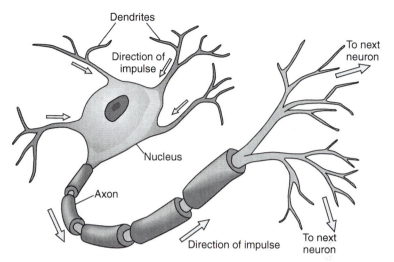

Figure 4.1 Basic schematic of a neuron.

Observation of a cross-section of a portion of the brain indicates neurons of different sizes connected together in an extremely complex network – some axons are very long, others very short; one neuron may connect to another which connects back to it in turn; the connections may be of completely different size and strength and, as discussed, may add to the threshold summation (excitatory) or subtract from it (inhibitory). Purely due to location, a lot of connections from one neuron are to nearby neurons, but some can be to neurons quite a distance away.

This structure arises partly for genetic reasons, due to the make-up of the brain of parents and ancestors, and partly from the brain development of the individual themselves, due to life experience. As an individual learns, the axon–dendrite connections in their brain strengthen (positively) or weaken (negatively), making the individual more or less likely to perform in a certain way. A brain is therefore extremely plastic in that it adapts and can function differently, dependent on the patterns of signals it receives and the rewards or punishments associated with them.

Doing something correctly in response to a particular event means that the neural pathways involved with the decision are likely to be strengthened, such that the next time the same event occurs, the brain is even more likely to make a similar choice. Meanwhile, doing something incorrectly in response to a particular event means that the neural pathways involved are likely to be weakened, such that next time that event occurs, the brain is less likely to make the same mistake!

This is the basis of biological brain growth, operation and development. It is ideas taken from both the structure of such a network and its method of learning that form the essential ingredients of an **artificial neural network** (ANN), the aim of which is to employ technological means to realise some of the characteristics of the original biological version.

Before taking a look at ANNs it is important to realise that it is, almost surely, not the aim to exactly copy an original biological brain, but rather to employ some of the ideas obtained from its method of operation in building the ANN. For a start, while the human brain has 100 billion cells, a typical ANN may have only a hundred or even less. This said, ANNs have been found to be extremely powerful and versatile AI tools capable of making decisions on, for example, rerouting power transmission lines, identifying forged signatures, recognising and understanding speech and spotting devious behaviour in credit card usage.

BASIC NEURON MODEL

We have already seen how a biological neuron works. A starting point for building an artificial network of neurons is to form a simple model of an individual neuron that can either be programmed into a computer – so that we can form an ANN by means of a computer program – or that can be built using electronic circuitry. In either case the overall aim is to build an ANN by connecting together lots of individual neuron models.

A neuron receives a number of signals on its inputs (its dendrites in the biological case), each one of which can be more or less influential. It adds these signals up and compares them with a threshold level. If the total sum is the same as or more than the threshold value then the neuron fires; if the sum is below the threshold then it does not fire. In this basic sense an artificial neuron operates in the same way as a biological neuron.

The neuron model shown in Figure 4.2 is commonly known as the McCulloch and Pitts model, named after the two scientists (Warren McCulloch and Walter Pitts) who proposed it in 1943. It operates as follows. The inputs x and y are multiplied by their associated weightings W_1 and W_2 and are summed together. The total is then compared to the bias value (b). The bias is effectively a negative value that the sum of the weighted inputs must surpass. So, if the sum of the weighted inputs is the same as or more than b, the neuron fires, giving an output of 1; if the sum is less than b, the neuron does not fire, giving an output of 0. The output can then be multiplied by its own further weighting before being in turn input to the next neuron.

As an example, assume that at some time, x is 2 and y is 1, W_1 is 2 and W_2 is −2, with the bias term b equal to 1. So W_1 multiplied by x is 4, whereas W_2 multiplied by y is −2, giving a sum of 2. Comparing the sum with the bias term b means that in this case the output would fire as 2 is greater than the value of b, which is 1 − i.e. the sum is more than the threshold.

Of course, we do not have to be limited to two inputs (in Figure 4.2 they are x and y); we can have any number, each one

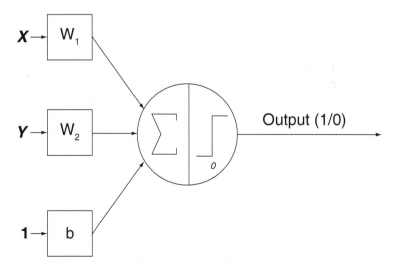

Figure 4.2 Basic model of a neuron.

being multiplied by their own weighting value. For the comparison with the threshold to occur, however, all of the inputs must first be multiplied by their respective weighting value before being summed.

Although the threshold action is very much like that of an actual neuron, it is just one possibility when it comes to describing the functioning of a neuron model. Another possibility exists if the output swings between 1 when fired and −1 (rather than 0) when not fired. This alternative model is just as plausible as they are both based on simple ideas from the operation of a biological neuron.

In fact, what appears to be the most popular choice, for research purposes, happens to use what is called a sigmoid (also called a leaky threshold) rather than a straightforward yes/no type of threshold. In this case, as the sum starts to increase, so the output will itself increase a little in value from its original 0, continuing to slowly increase as the sum increases, until its final value (1) is realised. Although this action is in fact less like that of an actual neuron it exhibits some nice mathematical characteristics which have been found to be useful. Essentially, the output travels more gently from 0 to 1 rather than being an immediate firing when the sum reaches exactly the threshold.

PERCEPTRONS AND LEARNING

The particular form of neuron model just described is referred to as a **perceptron**. Another way of looking at such a model (and using it in a practical way) is in terms of its ability to pigeon-hole pieces of information into particular classes (referred to as 'classifying'). In this sense, with any set of input values, the output of the neuron will be either 1 or −1, indicating to us that the input falls into one of two classes, Class 1, when the output is 1, or Class 2, when the output is −1.

When a perceptron has been set up appropriately it can be used to test inputs applied to assess whether they belong to Class 1 or Class 2. As an example, consider a (very) simple test to see if an applicant should receive a loan. Input x is 0 if they have never paid off a loan before and 1 if they have; input y is 0 if they have savings below some minimum and 1 if their savings are above the minimum. Let's assume that if an applicant satisfies the criteria both x and y being 1, then they will be given a loan, otherwise they will not.

One solution to this would be to make both weights, W_1 and W_2, equal to 2 and to have a bias term b of 3. To achieve the loan, both x and y would need to be 1 for the sum to reach 4 – a figure of greater than 3 – to achieve an output of 1, indicating Class 1. In this case, if x and/or y is zero the output for that item will be zero (0×2). This is referred to as the AND function as it needs both x AND y to be 1 for the output to be 1. In fact, with these same weights both equal to 2, simply lowering the threshold, b, to 1 means that the OR function is achieved in that, with the weights the same as before, when functioning in this way either x OR y OR both of them can be 1 for the output to be 1.

With only two inputs and one output the problem is not a particularly difficult one – this example was given merely to show how the perceptron can operate as a classifier. Even with only one perceptron it is quite possible for the number of inputs to be much higher, but with just one such neuron it is only possible to decide between two classes, nothing more complex, no matter how many inputs are applied. It is referred to as a **linearly separable problem**. If we wish to achieve a solution where lots of different classifications can be made, something referred to as linearly inseparable, then several perceptrons would need to be included – it is not possible with only one perceptron.

One issue, even with this simple case, is how we can know what weighting and bias values to use to obtain the classification action we want. For this we need a rule by which means the perceptron can learn – a technique to train the neuron's weights to satisfy the performance required from them. The idea is to start with any arbitrary selection of weights and for our learning technique, if it is a good one, to find for itself a set of weights that will provide the wanted solution by making small adjustments.

Let us consider training a perceptron to perform the AND function as an example. Assume the two inputs can only be either 0 or 1 and that the bias, b, is 3. For any particular set of inputs we know what we want the output to be – for the AND function when x is 1 AND y is 1 we want the output to be 1; for any other combination (e.g. when x is 1 and y is 0, the output will be 0). But assume initially that we do not know what value of weights, W_1 and W_2, are needed to achieve this. We need to find out.

Let us try some initial weights – a rough guess. Say W_1 is 1 and W_2 is 1, then the actual output found for the input pair (x is 1 and y is 1) would be 2, which is clearly less than the bias of 3, so the output would be 0, whereas we want it to be 1 – these weights are not a good choice. So, there is an error – our guess was not a good one. If we subtract the actual output (0) from the output we want (1) the resultant error is 1. We multiply the error by the inputs applied and add the result to the weight values selected to provide new weight values and then try the test again, so now the weights are both 2. When we try the inputs again we find this time the answer is correct – for these inputs, this selection of weights provides us with the function we wanted.

This process must normally be repeated with all the different input possibilities time and time again until eventually we find that the error has dropped to a very small value (hopefully zero) for all input possibilities, at which point the weights will be the correct ones for that input/output selection. It is useful when updating the weight values to also apply a value which signifies the rate of learning – the amount of updating can be either greater or, as is normal, much less than we used in the example. So the weight values would change much more slowly, eventually reaching a satisfactory solution.

For a simple example, as this one, it is not so critical what we choose for a learning rate factor, as long as it is somewhere between 0 and 1. A small number (e.g. 0.1) means the neuron will learn slowly, whereas a larger number (e.g. 0.5) means it will change (maybe too) quickly. Nevertheless, for the simple AND example here, no matter what initial weight selections we choose, after possibly six or seven adjustments over all of the input possibilities our weights should have settled down to a steady solution. Applying the weight update procedure described one more time will then result in no change in weight values. Indeed, this is often the best way to decide that learning has completed, in that the weight values do not change from one adjustment to the next (or at least change by a very small amount).

SELF-ORGANISING NEURAL NETWORK

Different parts of a brain carry out different functions. Various ANN schemes aim at copying, to a certain extent at least, some specific aspects of the brain's activity. One example is the area of the brain in humans, called the cerebral cortex, part of which deals with sensory input. In this region of the brain, sensory input is mapped to different regions of the cortex, which has organised itself to understand the variety of signals that arrive.

Ideas from this have been used in the development of a self-organising (winner-takes-all) ANN which consists of a single layer of neurons. Usually these do not have a strict threshold as has been previously described. They can operate on a more complex function, such as a sigmoid, but it might be best initially to consider them quite simply as outputting a value related to the sum of their input signals – possibly the sum itself.

These neurons are formed into a square matrix of possibly 100 neurons in a 10×10 array. The idea is that a particular input pattern will excite a specific region of the neurons in the array. In this way, when the network is operating, if it is witnessed that a particular region of the neurons is excited then the input pattern that caused this can be inferred, i.e. that particular piece of input information must have caused the output. The network is called a feature map in that by considering the different regions of the network, each region (when excited) infers that a particular input pattern, a feature, has been applied.

In this type of network, the same input signals – we have been considering two, x and y up to now, but there may well be more – are applied to all of the neurons in the array in exactly the same fashion. What is different here, however, is that the outputs from each of the neurons are also fed back to form further inputs to each of the neurons in turn – these are referred to as lateral connections.

Each of the signals applied to a neuron, both directly from the inputs themselves and also those fed back from neuron outputs, will have a weight associated with them. Initially these weights can be set to random values. When a particular input pattern is then applied, one of the (100) neurons will have an output signal which is higher than all the other neurons. This neuron is selected as the winner and its weights are adjusted to make its output even higher for that input pattern. In turn, the neurons in its vicinity also have their weights adjusted (but not quite so much) so that their outputs are also a little higher, and so on as we radiate out from the winning neuron, until neurons further away actually have their weights modified so that their outputs decrease.

For this reason the learning function is said to resemble a 'Mexican hat' shape, with the winning neuron at the centre/pinnacle of the hat and neurons further away on the brim. The hat shape defines how much an output is increased by a change of weights if it is close to the winning neuron, and how much the output is decreased when that neuron is further away. When trained in this way, if that specific input appears again then the neuron map will 'recognise' the input because the specific area around the winning neuron will be far more excited than the rest of the map.

Another input pattern is applied and a different neuron in another sector of the map is selected as the winner. Again, the Mexican hat learning function is employed in order to modify the weights, and as a result another area of the map will recognise this new input if it is applied again. This process is repeated with more, different inputs. In each case a new sector of the map is excited by the new input. So the map organises itself such that when training has been completed and the weights are fixed, the overall network can monitor a set of inputs such that when a particular input pattern is applied, or at least something close to it, one specific region of the neuron map will be excited.

It turns out that where there are some similarities or links between the different input signals then they are likely to excite adjacent regions of the neuron map. This means that if a sequence of input signals is applied, the result is that the area of excitation moves around the map as the inputs change.

Although such a map could be useful for recognising a whole range of different input types, one area of application in which it has been found to be successful is that of speech recognition. As a speech signal is input to the network – in terms of energy at different frequencies – phonemes can be recognised and the initial uttered words can be reconstructed from their frequency components by means of the map. Perhaps surprisingly, the Chinese language is one of the best to employ in such a test due to its logical phoneme structure.

N-TUPLE NETWORK

One final type of neural network we will consider here is the *N*-Tuple network, also referred to as a 'weightless' network because it operates in a distinctly different way, being (as one might guess) devoid of weights. Indeed, its principles of operation are substantially different to those looked at already and its method of learning is also dissimilar. However, in many ways it is a lot easier to actually build in electronics/hardware and possibly even to understand in terms of its mode of operation.

The basic building block (neuron) of an *N*-Tuple network is a standard computer random access memory (RAM) chip, as depicted in Figure 4.3. Further, for this technique all of the signals at both the input and output are binary, i.e. they are either 0 or 1 (no or yes). Such a restriction is not particularly limiting when it is remembered that when a signal is digitised, as required by a computer, then it is readily available in terms of 0s and 1s. The input connections to the neuron are actually the address lines of the RAM chip, and the output is the value of data (0 or 1) stored at that address.

When the RAM neuron is in learning mode, the pattern being taught is input in terms of 1s and 0s on the memory address lines, with the appropriate value being stored – either 1

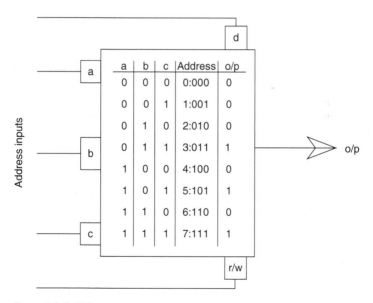

Figure 4.3 RAM neuron.

or 0. The number of inputs used to address the RAM neuron is referred to as a Tuple – if there are eight bits (eight 0s and 1s) then this would be an 8-Tuple. Subsequently, when in analysis mode, the neuron is addressed with the same input pattern and the data extracted will be either the 1 or 0 that was previously learnt. This is essentially a different – yet powerful – way of employing a RAM chip.

This type of neuron can be particularly useful for learning to recognise an image. If the image is split up into pixels, with each pixel having a value either of 1 or 0, then the pixels can be taken four at a time (if it is a 4-Tuple network) and fed into RAM neurons. Different RAM neurons are required for each Tuple.

To see how it works, let us initially store a 0 as data for all possible addresses in a RAM neuron. Then assume that we have an image which simply consists of four pixels, with each pixel either being black (0) or white (1). For this example let us say the four pixels will have value 1010 and a RAM neuron will be so addressed, with a 1 being stored at that address.

If we subsequently test the neuron with an image 1011 then the neuron will output 0, indicating that it does not recognise that image. If, however, we input an image 1010 then the neuron will output 1, indicating that it does recognise that image as the one it originally learnt.

Of course, a typical image consists of many more pixels than this, even with merely a black and white image. So a whole bank of such neurons are needed, with every pixel being fed into at least one neuron, although it is usual to over-sample and feed each (0/1) pixel value into four or more different neurons, often in a pseudo-random way in order to generalise and mix up the inputs. For a particular image, the first N bits are fed into the first neuron, the second N bits into the next neuron and so on until the whole image input pattern has been dealt with.

For a specific image fed into the neurons in this way, all of the neurons have their outputs set to 1 for this particular pattern. In this case, because so many neurons are involved, when it comes to the analysis stage and a subsequent image is presented, because of small changes such as light discrepancies or noise, the image will probably not be exactly the same at any later time – it may be that for what we think is the same image, only 83% of the neurons give a 1 as output. In fact, this is probably near enough. Because the percentage is so high, it is likely the case that the image is just about the same as the one originally learnt. If only 25% of the outputs had given a 1 as output then we could be pretty sure that it was a different image to the first one.

For a bank of neurons, therefore, we simply need to sum up all of the outputs and make a judgement ourselves as to what value we feel is sufficient to convince us that the image is near enough to the original.

In practice it is best for the neurons not simply to learn one specific image but to learn a number of similar images.

If the neurons were learning to recognise the image taken of a person's face, for example, it might be that the person could move their head slightly or open and close their mouth, with a different image fed in to the bank of neurons in each case – each of the different images causing some extra neurons to have their data lines set to 1. Subsequently, the sum of neuron outputs would then be more likely to give a high percentage value even if the person's head was not in exactly the same position as it was at first – possibly due to the wind blowing their hair or the sun reflecting differently.

One issue is that if too many different images are learnt by a bank of such neurons, then in analysis mode it tends to recognise absolutely everything it is tested with – its discrimination is impaired. It is usual, therefore, to have a different bank of RAM neurons for each different image, with slight variations on that image. For this reason, such a bank of neurons is referred to as a 'discriminator'. If it is, at a later time, desired to clear the entire discriminator and teach it a completely new input pattern then it is relatively straightforward to simply set all neuron outputs for all address inputs to 0 and start again.

It is clear that RAM neurons are not a particularly accurate model of a human neuron. However, their performance in input (particularly image) recognition has certainly been inspired by the neural processes of the human brain – as a result such performance itself results in further questions being asked as to the actual nature of human neurons themselves – perhaps, in some cases, they are more like the RAM neurons than we initially thought.

EVOLUTIONARY COMPUTING

In Chapter 2 we considered problem solving in terms of searching for a solution. Various search techniques were investigated. In recent years inspiration has been taken from the study of biological evolution to provide an alternative, very powerful strategy when it is required to search for a – possibly the best – solution to a problem by selecting from a number of potential solutions. Even, if required, realising new solutions not previously considered – i.e. being creative.

In the biological evolutionary process, at one point in time a population of individuals in a species exists, forming a generation. These individuals are mixed together (usually by mating) to produce a new generation, and so over time the species survives and (hopefully) thrives. As the environment changes, to stay in existence the species must adapt to those changes. But this overall process is extremely slow, possibly taking millions of years.

By copying (modelling) in a computer some of the general processes involved in the biological form of evolution, it is possible to achieve a technique which adapts (improves) the solution to an AI problem, from a population of potential solutions, either towards the best possible solution or at least to achieve a solution that works.

Different solutions in one generation of the population of solutions are mixed (genetically by mating) to produce a new, improved generation. The solutions in that new generation can in turn be mixed, in a number of ways, to realise the next generation and so on, until many – possibly thousands – of generations later a much better solution to the original problem is arrived at. Fortunately, computer generations can be brought about within a much shorter time frame – possibly seconds or even milliseconds – so we don't have to wait millions of years for a solution to appear.

GENETIC ALGORITHMS

The best-known approach to evolutionary computing is the method of genetic algorithms (GAs). In this technique, each member of a population is defined in terms of a genetic make-up (computer chromosomes) which describes it uniquely. This can be written in binary fashion, in terms of 1s and 0s. To get from one generation to the next, the chromosomes of one member are mixed/mated with those of another by procedures such as crossover and mutation, which were inspired by their biological counterparts.

As we will see, a binary chromosome code relates directly to the characteristics of each member. Differences between members' chromosomes relate to the actual differences between their properties. As a simple example, one member – let's say A – may be described by the code 0101, whereas another – we'll call it B – could be described by 1100. The process of crossover involves taking part of the code of A and mixing it with part of the code of B to make a new member for the next generation. For example, the first part (first two digits) of A mixed with the second part (last two digits) of B would realise 0100 – a new code. For longer codes, which is the usual case, the process is exactly the same; it's just that more digits are involved.

Mutation, which is generally used less frequently, involves taking one digit (possibly at random) and changing it. So we might take A as 0101 and mutate this by changing the third digit for it to become 0111 in the next generation. In a piece of code with only four digits, as in our example, this has quite a dramatic effect, whereas if only one digit is mutated out of a 24-digit code description then the effect is much less apparent.

It needs to be remembered here that the original members of the population might well be quite reasonable solutions in any case, so we most likely would not wish to change them much from one generation to the next, just some small tweaks to improve them slightly. In nature, mutation occurs sparingly and this is perhaps the best case with a GA also – in fact, too much mutation can seriously disrupt a GA, leading to it never finding a good solution.

When operating a GA, the first task is to construct fixed-length chromosomes which are representative of the problem and which uniquely characterise each individual in the total population. Also, one needs to choose a population size and decide if this is going to be allowed to grow in any way (probably not). When the population size is fixed from generation to generation it means that some of the entities in a generation will need to be killed off – i.e. they will not proceed further. They will most likely be the weakest individuals, though it may be that some diversity is required and hence individuals that are very similar to others, but not quite as good, can be killed off along with clones – a population full of identical individuals is not desirable.

It also needs to be decided how much crossover and how much mutation will occur. The probability of either of these occurring can usually be determined from experience with a particular problem – too much of either and the population will not settle down and converge on a good solution; not enough of either and the population can get trapped with only bad solutions.

Perhaps the most important aspect is determining how the individuals are to be measured – what is good and what is bad. For this an overall function which defines the fitness of individuals needs to be constructed (a **fitness function**). This depends on the problem for which the GA is being applied. The function may therefore be arrived at by a combination of different factors – e.g. speed, cost, power or length, whatever is important for the problem.

To start the algorithm off, an initial population is required. This might be obtained randomly or it could be obtained through a number of rough guesses at a solution. The fitness of each member of the first generation in the population is found by means of the fitness function. A pair of chromosomes can then be selected for mating – those achieving a better fitness score are more likely to mate. Crossover and mutation operators are applied depending on their probability in each case. As a result, one or more offspring are produced. This process may well then be repeated with other pairs of chromosomes.

What results is a new population consisting of the original chromosomes and the new offspring. Each of the chromosomes is then tested against the fitness function and the population is slimmed down to the population size by killing off some chromosomes (simply eliminating them from the proceedings). These chromosomes take no further part in the process. The fitness function may indeed include a factor dependent on age, such that for each generation a chromosome may be deemed a little less fit simply because it is ageing. This aspect depends on the application, however, and it may be that chromosome age is not deemed important.

This whole process is repeated, generation after generation – possibly many thousands of generations – until there is little or no change in the fitness function calculations for the best chromosomes. At this point it can be deemed that a solution has been arrived at.

Sometimes it may be that there is little change in the best chromosome's fitness function calculation for several generations – indeed, the value may deteriorate – and then it can start to improve again. It really depends on the complexity of the problem. It could therefore be that it is simply better to stop the algorithm after a specified number of generations have been realised or when the best fitness reaches a certain value – the result will then be deemed to be 'good enough'.

GENETIC ALGORITHM: SIMPLE EXAMPLE

In this simple example we wish to use a GA to find the best robot to perform a package carrying task. The robot can have one of two motors, one of two chassis, one of two power supplies and one of two grippers. For the first type of each item this will be denoted by 0, with the second type denoted by 1. Let's have a population of three possible robots and let's start them off as 1010, 0111 and 1000. Each of these chromosomes actually represents a different physical robot made up of the four different possible components.

Each robot performs in terms of speed (S), manoeuvrability (M) and load carrying (L), due to the way it is constructed. Our fitness function (F) can therefore be made up of some aspects of each of these features – let's say $F = xS + yM + zL$, where x, y and z are numbers we choose to denote the importance of each feature. In the first generation we calculate F for each of the three robots – to do so we need a mathematical model which relates S, L and M to each of the robot designs. Assume that, as a result, we find that 1010 and 0111 have better values of F. We then apply crossover to these to obtain 1011 and subsequently apply mutation to the third digit of 0111 to obtain an offspring 0101.

On testing it is found that 1000 from the original population and 1011 have the worst fitness functions (F) – so our population at the start of the second generation consists of 1010 and 0111 from the original population, along with the offspring 0101.

Now we test each of these robots against F using the model (which we assume we have) and find that 0111 and 0101 are the best two in this case. Applying crossover gives us 0101 again, while applying mutation to the fourth digit of the first of these (0111) gives us 0110. As a result, we find the new population of three robots to be 0111, 0101 and 0110.

So the process continues. Perhaps we eventually find that 0110 turns out to be the best solution in terms of satisfying the fitness function and we simply cannot obtain a better design of robot. In this case we have found the components we need to build the actual, physical robot, which we can go ahead and do.

One of the first tests for the robot will be to check its actual speed, manoeuvrability and load-carrying performance. In this way the mathematical model relating these features to the actual robot components (which we assumed we already had) can be checked. If the model is found to accurately relate to the actual performance characteristics then we can be pretty sure that the GA has found the best solution for the design of the robot. If, however, the model is found to be in error, then it may be the case that a different fitness function would have been better and that the GA has found the right solution to the wrong problem. What is needed, though, is a more accurate model so that the fitness function is more realistic.

This example points to a number of important characteristics inherent in the use of GAs for problem solving. First, the chromosomes must accurately represent the individuals – in the case of the robot the motor, gripper and so on must be accurately represented. Second, the fitness function must accurately be related to the performance of the individuals in the population.

In a realistic version of a problem such as this, each chromosome could be made up of 20 or more digits (not four as in the example), the population might contain hundreds of different chromosomes (not just the three in the example) and the fitness function could represent a complex mathematical description relating each individual's make-up to its performance, consisting of many more than the three terms in the example.

GENETIC ALGORITHMS: SOME COMMENTS

In natural selection, individuals who are not so fit in terms of their performance do not survive; as they age, they die off. Although this was originally referred to as 'survival of the fittest', perhaps a better description might be non-survival of the unfit. Those that are fit enough survive and mate, and in that fashion pass on their genes to the next generation. In many ways, GAs are based on the same principles. For example, the chromosome size (length) does not change from generation to generation.

One difference with nature is that the size of a GA population normally remains fixed. This is rather akin to managing a group of animals on a wildlife reservation – the strongest animals survive and the weakest and/or oldest are culled. The main reason for retaining population size in a GA is simply management of the algorithm – letting the size expand would mean that for each generation, the fitness function for every individual would have to be calculated, which takes up computer time, so as generations passed the amount of computation time required would increase considerably.

However, restricting the population size in a GA, while helping on time, does create problems. What can tend to happen is that individuals in the population can become similar, leading to a lack of diversity. If we wish to find the best solution it can be good to have some different individuals in the population to vary the solution to an extent.

In some instances the GA can be operated adaptively to deal with changing circumstances, such as when a robot has to deal with different environmental conditions. In these cases diversity in the population is important such that quite large changes in individuals can occur if and when necessary, relatively quickly.

Although the desire is for a GA to find the overall (global) best solution, it may be that there are several potential solutions, some of them better than others. This situation occurs when the fitness function is quite complex. It is then possible for the GA to converge on a local maximum rather than the global solution. It can be that a different start point (i.e. different initial conditions) will allow the global solution to be found, but there again we don't know what those conditions are if we don't know the final/global solution.

In biological evolution local maxima can in some circumstances be good solutions. Such is the case for different species that have developed to fill a niche for which they physically and mentally evolve with specific characteristics to deal with a particular situation. This same feature may also be useful with some GA applications, with the GA providing a neat solution to a specific problem.

In essence, whether we are looking at a niche solution – a good thing – or merely a local maximum – possibly not such a good thing – really depends on the particular application.

AGENT METHODS

If we take a look at the general approach to AI discussed in this chapter so far it is one of the emergence of an overall complex intelligent behaviour through a collection of simpler interacting entities which are, themselves, semi-autonomous – *agents*. It may be, as we have seen with ANNs, that these agents, in the form of neurons, merely link together and, by their sheer numbers achieve intelligent behaviour. Alternatively, as we have seen with GAs, it may be that a population of genes, as agents, improves through an evolutionary process with an external assessor – the fitness function.

In either case we can see that each agent has little/no knowledge of what other agents do. They are relatively independent and are only affected, in turn, by other agents in terms of achieving environmental goals. An end result may then be realised in terms of one agent alone (in the case of a GA) or by a collection or community of agents (in the case of an ANN).

One approach to AI is to specifically focus on the idea of agents in particular and their individual identities to produce an overall emergent behaviour. Each element can be considered as a member of a society that can usually perceive limited aspects of its environment, which it can in turn affect either singly or in cooperation with other agents. In this way an agent coordinates with other agents to achieve a specific task. A key difference between this approach and classical AI is that with agents the overall intelligence is distributed between the agents rather than being housed in one centralised depository.

AGENTS FOR PROBLEM SOLVING

We saw in Chapter 2 how classical AI systems can be very good at solving problems. An alternative solution is to employ an agent-based approach. In this way a complex problem can be chopped up into a number of smaller problems, each one of which is much easier to deal with. Agents can then be used to find solutions to these smaller problems – combining together to realise the final solution. One advantage of this is that each agent can contain information about its own smaller problem – it doesn't need to know anything about the problem in general.

Such an approach is often taken between humans to tackle a difficult task, each human only dealing with their specific part of the problem, usually not understanding the full complexity of the overall situation. So it seems quite reasonable to apply the same technique to an AI system. But of course, there are many different ways in which this can be brought about. As such, you will encounter several different definitions of what an agent is and what it can do.

Some agents have a fixed action, while others are flexible and adaptive. Some are autonomous, while some are completely dependent on the decisions of others. Most are responsive to the environment in which they exist, although this can mean environment in the sense of the outside world or it can mean the actions of other surrounding agents – think of one of your neurons in the middle of your brain, for example – it is only affected by other neurons, not directly by any external influence.

It may be that in a particular design all agents have the same power and capabilities; however, it may be that some agents can override the decisions of others – this is referred to as **subsumption architecture** as the action or decision of one, lower-priority agent is subsumed by that of an agent of higher priority. As an example, we will shortly consider this further in terms of a mobile robot application.

SOFTWARE AGENTS

An agent can take the form of a physical hardware entity or it can be a piece of code in the computer as part of an overall program. In either case it exhibits some or all of the characteristics already discussed. In a moment we will look at hardware agents. First, however, let us consider the software version.

There are a wide range of possible software agents – sometimes referred to as softbots. For example, such agents are presently used to monitor the financial markets, checking on the real-time movements of stocks and share prices. An agent may well be responsible for buying and selling commodities, in which case it needs to know if the (human) dealer has any up-to-the-minute instructions as to which trades it should be especially interested in and which to avoid – in this case the agent may need to 'understand' certain natural language instructions.

Agents are ideal for such transactions because they can simply sit monitoring activity, only carrying out an action when the right conditions are apparent. Not only is this very difficult for a human to do, but once a decision is needed the agent can make it almost instantly. In the time it would take for a human broker to make the same decision (several seconds or even minutes) the deal may well have been lost.

As a result, a large proportion of daily financial transactions around the world are actually carried out, not by humans, but by software agents. The office floors of financial houses in the city market places (London/New York) are smothered in computers. Brokers that formerly were involved in carrying out the transactions are now involved in monitoring AI agents and feeding them with information and occasionally instructions – then they let them get on with it. Meanwhile, others are involved in new AI agent design – it is no longer the company making the best deals that makes the money, but rather the company that realises the best AI agents.

Such an agent may well monitor numerous factors at the same time: keeping a historical record of the value of shares over a period; investigating trends; correlating these with other shares; linking them with financial exchange rates and other external information translated from up-to-date news items. As many factors are brought together it may be that some of the data mining techniques discussed earlier need to be either directly incorporated into an agent or the agent needs access as and when it is required.

The basic action of an agent is to take in information from one or a number of inputs, process this information, relate it to historical data and to make a decision which can be acted on either physically or in terms of a further software output, possibly even by another agent. This could be achieved simply through the agent consisting of a rule base or a look-up table. If historical data is ignored then the agent is referred to as a **reflex agent**.

It may be that the agent contains elements concerned with planning in order to achieve either an internal goal or to direct itself towards an external goal – in which case it is referred to as a **goal-based agent**. Meanwhile, if the planning elements themselves are adapted appropriately in response to external influences from the environment, possibly due to the performance of the agent itself, then this is referred to as a **learning agent**. Finally, an agent can be based on models obtained from the real world, which it attempts to mimic in its performance, in which case it is referred to as a **model-based agent**.

MULTIAGENTS

We have looked thus far more at single agents acting, in some way, as a part of a collective whole. It may well be in some cases that a single agent is required to deal with a task (many industrial monitoring systems are of this ilk), merely checking on a measured level, pressure or flow and sounding an alarm or triggering a valve to open/close if the measured value deviates outside previously defined bounds.

If a single agent is appropriate to deal with a problem, then so be it – there is no point making the solution more complex than it needs to be. However, there are many cases in which a number of agents are required; in fact, it is more than likely that this will be the case as it is such situations in which AI agent systems are applied.

Where **multiagents** are involved they may need to operate in a cooperative fashion such that each agent provides a partial answer to a problem, an overall solution being provided by bringing together the cohesive outputs from a number of agents. Alternatively, the agents may operate competitively, either singly or in groups, with only one or a small group of active agents providing the final overall solution.

To deal with multiagent systems, a form of selection is required. This can be carried out either in terms of a simple calculation; for example, each agent can be assigned a priority grading (can be called an ego), with such gradings being merely added together if groups of agents are involved. The winning active agent(s) is then the one(s) with the 'best' grading. Alternatively, a critic or superagent is also required in order to choose, by means of its comparative calculations, which is the winning agent to be applied. The superagent itself does not therefore affect the outside world; its role is to select which agents can do so.

HARDWARE AGENTS

Historically, computer systems were fed information by users. In many cases this is still true. However, it is also the case that many computer systems (acting as agents) obtain their information directly from sensing the environment and are both expected and trusted to act on that information without any form of human intervention. The result of this may well mean the actuation of some entity which directly affects and influences the real world. As an example, a peacekeeper missile system receives information regarding incoming enemy missiles and their range and trajectory. The AI system itself then decides when to deploy a missile – humans merely have a veto but no direct control.

The computer system requires an accurate up-to-date picture of the state of the external world. If it senses inaccurate information then any decisions it makes will themselves be inaccurate. Such data, on collection, may need processing to reduce the possibility of error, so data may need to be averaged or filtered to remove noise. One good example of a computer/agent system operating in this way is the case of a mobile robot. The robot senses information related to its position and whether any objects are in its vicinity. It may then need to plan a course of action and subsequently attempt to carry out that action, taking into account any environmental changes or newly sensed information – maybe an object has suddenly appeared in front of it.

Such a robot can also learn a reliable procedure or behaviour depending on potential actions it tries itself being 'rewarded' when it gets things right and 'punished' when it gets things wrong. We will look at this in more detail in the next chapter.

SUBSUMPTION ARCHITECTURE

In order to describe the subsumption architecture method, it is best to stick with the mobile robot as our example agent because the robot has a number of levels of operation. At one level the robot may need to form a map of its environment – in practice this may be by means of a laser range-finding mechanism or perhaps ultrasonic sensors. In order to do this it will need to move around in the environment.

Another task the robot might have is to go to one point on the map to take an object from that point to another point. Of course, the desire would probably be that if any objects get in its way then it must avoid them (in an industrial setting) or possibly destroy them (in a military setting). It might be, however, that its role will change depending on the object sensed and the function the object is carrying out. Hence, it might be required that on encountering a specific object, the robot stops taking its load from one place to another, changes its direction and goes somewhere else.

Each of the tasks of the robot has a level of required competence – avoiding collisions is of high priority but requires a low competence. Following a path requires a high competence but is not so high in terms of priority. Other functions of the robot can similarly be defined, such as building a map, travelling relatively aimlessly, sensing changes in the environment and so on.

Overall, at any point in time, the robot will be collecting data but will also need to decide on a course of action for that point in time – what does it do? To this end the controller has several layers of action, each with its own level of competence and each with its own priority. It is important that at each point in time there will be only one selected action.

It will most likely be the case that a number of possible actions are active – maybe the robot is presently carrying an object from one place to another (high competence) when it encounters an object blocking its path requiring avoidance (low competence).

The basic rules of subsumption architecture are that: first, a lower competence action will always subsume (or suppress) a higher competence action; second, the 'default behaviour' is always the lowest competence one. In this way different levels of possible action are subsumed into the immediate, necessary action which simply must be taken.

CONCLUDING REMARKS

In this chapter we have looked at some of the modern approaches to AI. In doing so we have taken more of a bottom-up approach, looking at the basic building blocks of intelligence and investigating how these can be plugged together, rather like the neurons in our brains, in order to function as an intelligent collective whole. This is in direct contrast to classical AI in which an external, top-down approach is taken.

As we have travelled through the chapter, so ANNs, evolutionary computing and agent architectures have all been considered, each with their own distinctly different mode of operation. We have seen that robotics has proved to be a good example to consider where and how AI systems operate. As a result we will continue our investigation into AI by looking at robots in more detail, considering how they sense the world and operate within it, focusing on how they exhibit intelligence in the form of AI.

KEY TERMS

artificial neural network, fitness function, goal-based agent, learning agent, linearly separable problem, model-based agent, multi-agents, perceptron, reflex agent, subsumption architecture

FURTHER READING

1   *Bio-inspired Artificial Intelligence: Theories, Methods and Technologies* by D. Floreano and C. Mattiussi, published by MIT Press, 2008. This is well written with many highly informative examples from biology, engineering and computing. It provides excellent coverage of the bio-inspired area.

2   *Neural Networks for Pattern Recognition* by C.M. Bishop, published by Clarendon Press, 1996. A very popular book for good reason. It offers comprehensive coverage of all types of neural networks, and has a pattern-recognition theme.

3   *Neural Networks and Learning Machines* by S. Haykin, published by Pearson Education, 2008. This is quite simply the best book on neural networks. It is a thorough, readable edition focusing mainly on an engineering approach.

4   *Introduction to Evolutionary Computing* by A.E. Eiben and J.E. Smith, published by Springer, 2010. This book provides a complete overview of evolutionary computing based on the principles of biological evolution, such as natural selection and

genetic inheritance. It is meant for those who wish to apply evolutionary computing to a particular problem or within a given application area. It contains quick-reference information on the current state-of-the-art.

5 *Soft Computing: Integrating Evolutionary, Neural and Fuzzy Systems* by A. Tettamanzi, M. Tomassini and J. Janßen, published by Springer, 2010. This is more for engineering or applied science students, and contains many application examples.

5

ROBOTS

SYNOPSIS

Some of the most exciting developments in the field of AI have appeared through the development of robotics. Indeed, it could be argued that an intelligent robot is merely the embodiment of an artificially intelligent entity – giving a body to AI. Topics to be covered here include artificial life, collective and swarm intelligence, and biologically inspired techniques. However, we also look at an exciting new form of AI in the sense of growing biological brains, as the AI, within a physical robot body. This can even mean culturing human brain cells as the AI!

ARTIFICIAL LIFE

In Chapter 1, when we were trying to pin down intelligence by defining it, the proposal was: 'The variety of information-processing processes that collectively enable a being to autonomously pursue its survival.' At first glance this definition can appear a bit bland – a similar, but more direct alternative might be: 'The variety of mental processes that act together to make up those necessary for life.' Again, we are looking here at a general, all-encompassing concept rather than something that is specific to (or biased towards) humans. However, in this latter definition we have tied intelligence to being something to do with mental (of the mind) processes, but more importantly have given it a central role in terms of life and living entities, including properties such as success and gain as well as mere survival.

Immediately, though, we can expect to have follow-up questions as to what is meant by 'the mind' and, somewhat more importantly, what is meant by 'life'? In Chapter 3 we attempted to tackle some of the philosophical arguments that relate to what a mind is and how a computer mind compares with a human mind. It is, however, relatively straightforward to regard a mind as merely being a brain, a physical entity which carries out the mental processes exhibited by an intelligent being. In this sense, discussing what a 'mind' is becomes more of a fun parlour game – the real question relates to what life is all about.

We can, as we did in Chapter 1 with regard to intelligence, have a look at what dictionaries say about life. However, arguably the best definition one finds is actually taken from Wikipedia and can be expressed succinctly by saying that life is a characteristic that distinguishes entities that have self-sustaining processes from those that do not.

In terms of a biological perspective, these self-sustaining processes for an entity involve regulation of its internal environment, organisation in itself, metabolism (e.g. energy), growth, adaptability, response to stimuli, production (not 'reproduction' – as mentioned earlier, humans do not reproduce other than in cloning) and other things such as excretion and nutrition, which are perhaps subsets of the previous categories.

So, to be considered to be alive an entity must exhibit the majority, if not all, of the characteristics mentioned – to go further we would be defining a specific form of life, such as organic or human, and in this look at AI we are trying to take a general approach to life, just as we are taking a general approach to intelligence. As with our analysis of intelligence, it is worth thinking about the variety of entities we witness on our planet when we consider life. It is certainly not necessary to exhibit ALL of the processes mentioned to be alive – for example, not all humans produce offspring, but this doesn't mean they are not alive.

A-LIFE

Having considered, to some extent at least, what life is all about, we can now look at the exciting topic of **artificial life**, otherwise known as A-life. This can mean a number of things to different people, depending on the approach being taken. However, what is common between these approaches is that some aspects of life as we know it are taken as the basis (or inspiration) for the A-life study.

Essentially, what happens in life can be modelled and used as a basis, or inspiration, for an AI technique. Alternatively, the role of an AI system can be to perform some or all aspects of life itself – which can be in terms of hardware (e.g. an actual physical robot) or in terms of a computer simulation of a world within the computer. In the latter case this can mean an attempt at representing the real world or it can be merely in terms of a toy/virtual world within software.

A-life approach 1 (merely inspirational): in the previous chapter we looked at neural networks, evolutionary computing, GAs and software agents. These computing AI methods are all inspired by a look at what happens in nature, either (as in the case of a neural network) how a brain works or (as in the case of evolutionary computing) how life evolves. Whether it be in terms merely of computer simulations of these forms of AI, to some people such techniques are considered to be part of the field of A-life.

A-life approach 2 (again merely inspirational): other, different aspects of life can be picked on and employed along with more standard forms of AI of the type considered in earlier chapters (e.g. planning) to improve performance or simply to take a different approach. Examples of this would be the use of models of social and cultural change to affect what would be otherwise standard forms of machine learning. In common with GAs, an attempt is made to cause a resultant behaviour to emerge through a perceived evolutionary process. This can be achieved in a simple way through merely having a number of potential solutions to a problem, being able to put a value on each solution and progressively (in an evolving way) to improve the best solution selected.

SIMULATED A-LIFE

What I have described so far is merely the use of inspirational ideas, gleaned from life, to influence the way either classical or modern AI methods operate. On first encountering the term 'artificial life', however, the immediate concept that would probably spring up in most people's minds is not this at all, but rather the idea of actually putting together/building an artificial life form. This is something that could be in terms of a simulation or in terms of a real-world, physical robot.

A simulated A-life can be quite complex (possibly a model of some aspects of life), containing behavioural models of individuals living within a simulated world, or it can be very simple in its construction. The amazing thing is that even with simple rules and simple behaviours, extremely complex overall population effects can arise.

CELLULAR AUTOMATA

Perhaps the best example of simulated A-life is the approach called **cellular automata** (also known as finite-state machines). One straightforward way to understand this is to consider a chess/draughts board as the simulated world, but in this case each of the squares can be either black or white and their status can change over time. Each square (described as a cell) is then considered to be an individual member of the world, which is the board itself.

If we consider a square in the middle of the board, it has eight neighbouring squares, four to the north (N), south (S), east (E) and west (W), and also four to the northwest (NW), northeast (NE), southwest (SW) and southeast (SE). At a specific time (t) then that square (in our simulated world) will be either black or white, which we can also call being in the state 1 or 0.

If we then consider the same square the next time we look at it ($t+1$) then its state at the new time will depend both on what its own state was at time t and what the state of its neighbours was at time t. At the next time ($t+2$) so things will depend on the states at time $t+1$, and so on.

Although this sounds a very simple operational description, when viewed over a sequence of such time steps, extremely complex patterns can emerge dependent on the choice of relationships between an individual square at a certain time, its previous self and its previous neighbours. Essentially, complexity emerges from simple behaviours even when the population (in this case the total number of squares) is relatively small.

What such a relatively simple set up does allow us to do is to study the effects of society, in that the state of an individual not only depends on itself but also on those around it. The type of relationships between a single cell and its surrounding cells can take a variety of forms, as we will see shortly, and in certain circumstances this can lead to cell 'death'. In this sense, 'death' means that a cell no longer changes its state over time and no longer has an effect on other cells around it – the speed with which this occurs (if it occurs) depends on the relationships themselves.

One thing that transpires from such a study is that the evolution of the total population over time, including the patterns that emerge, may not have an 'intent' about it (i.e. there may be no apparent, selected goal for the population), but rather a supposed 'intent' emerges from the simple interactions between the cells (i.e. regular patterns clearly emerge).

Conclusions from this can be drawn and posed back on our own human society. For example, such evolution may well not result in a 'better' existence (a better pattern) but merely a different one. Perhaps more importantly, mere survival seems to be the key factor (for a cell) – as long as you survive then you still have a role to play and can change things – this can be considered to be success in itself.

GAME OF LIFE

In looking at cellular automata it is worth considering how such evolutionary behaviour can occur in terms of a simple example. To start with, let's look again at a cell (square) in the middle of the board, along with its eight near neighbours. We need to define the relationships which will transform the state of the cell from time t to time $t+1$. For this example, let us merely use three rules to encompass the whole arrangement.

1 If a cell is in state 1 at time t and has exactly two (no more, no less) of its neighbours also in state 1 at time t, then at time $t+1$ it will remain in state 1.
2 Whatever the state of a cell at time t, if exactly three (no more, no less) of its eight neighbours are in state 1 at time t, then at time $t+1$ it will be in state 1.
3 For any other situation at time t, then at time $t+1$ the cell will be in state 0.

Consider for a moment the meaning of the rules in this example. If two or three neighbouring cells are 1 then the cell will itself result as a 1, whereas if more than three or less than two neighbouring cells are 1 then the cell itself will result as a 0. The cell needs just the right amount of activity around it – too much or too little and it will become 0. Even with such a simple set of rules, which all cells adhere to, seemingly rich and complex patterns can emerge in the population as a whole.

To see what can happen over just one time step with these rules it is worth simply drawing out a small grid (say 5×5), scattering some 1s and 0s around the grid and applying the rules repeatedly over a small number of time steps. From this it should be apparent that, dependent on the initial set up you selected, the grid may well, in this case, quickly fill up entirely with 0s or 1s or could, very quickly, simply become a stable, non-changing pattern. On further study it is realised that a larger population with a more diverse initial arrangement can easily lead to more complex patterns forming over time, possibly with waves, repeated cycles and shape changes.

WRAP-AROUND

It is quite straightforward, computationally, to extend the two-dimensional world cell picture considered thus far by operating a wrap-around policy. In the simple two-dimensional board case, the cells along an edge only have five neighbours. These cells either need to be given slightly different rules or their status will most likely have a biasing effect on the whole population.

It can be best for a cell on the right-hand edge to regard those respective cells on the left-hand edge as its neighbours and vice versa, with the same applying to cells on the top/bottom. Cells in the corner positions of a two-dimensional board meanwhile would nominally only have three neighbours. Wrapping around a corner cell in terms of right/left and top/bottom realises a further two neighbours in each case. Such corner cells therefore need to be wrapped around diagonally such that the opposite diagonal corner cell will also be a neighbour. In this way a corner cell will have all three other corner cells considered as its neighbours.

Interestingly, when wrap-around is applied, waves and what are termed 'gliders' (apparent objects with evolving shape) can move across the world and disappear off one edge only to reappear on the opposite edge. It is possible, in this way, to get gliders to continually circle the world in a stable, time-locked loop.

REAL-LIFE MODIFICATION

Just as AI can take inspiration from the real world in terms of its construction and operation, the same is true with A-life. However, it is also apparent that results from A-life can make us think in an alternate way about real life and our understanding of evolution. This is particularly true because of the 'bottom-up' aspect of A-life, in that simple individual cells realise a complex overall social and evolutionary behaviour simply through their interaction.

With cellular automata, a small change to individual cell rules, particularly in terms of how they are affected by their neighbours, can often result in distinctly different population developments, leading to a conclusion that in the real world if we all behaved slightly differently then the human race would realise very different outputs and evolve differently.

One input from the field of A-life to other subject areas is to stimulate a simplistic view of what may at first appear to be complex behaviour. Whatever the field (e.g. biology, physics, chemistry), an approach to studying complex behaviour as observed in those fields can be to try to realise a similar behaviour in terms of simple (cell) interactive behaviours. If this is possible, approximately at least, then it may be possible to modify the complex behaviour more to what we want by changing the cell behaviour.

REAL-LIFE INSPIRATION

What we have considered thus far in terms of cellular automata has involved all cells having the same set of (relatively simple) rules and behaving in exactly the same way. If we study a group of ants, for example, it may be that we conclude that all ants (or groups of ants at least) behave in the same sort of way. We can therefore draw an analogy between the ants and our game of life in that just as we see complex societal effects resulting from our simple cellular automata, so we see complex population output from a group of ants.

In both cases the population may appear to exhibit an overall goal or driving force as a result of the individual behaviour of its members.

But if we consider instead populations that we can perhaps understand (at least we think we understand) a little more about, such as humans, then we can see immediately that we may well need to change our specific set of rules for each individual and even groups of individuals in one or a number of ways, some of which are:

1 Different cells can operate on different sets of rules.
2 Groups of cells can operate with similar/collective rules. Such cells can be positioned geographically adjacent or can be scattered over the population in a structured or unstructured way.
3 Rules for cells can change as time progresses. In this way learning can be incorporated.
4 Rule sets can be goal directed, even on an individual basis. Different cells can have different goals.
5 Not all cells need to be updated on every time step.
6 Related to point 5, some cells can be updated every second or third time step, although this update frequency can change with respect to time.
7 A cell's update in terms of its neighbours' status can be quite different, resulting in either a much simpler or more complex rule set. For example, a cell could be affected by its neighbours' neighbours, or it could be affected by cells which are not geographically local, or it could be affected by only a select number of its neighbours – perhaps those at NW, NE, SW and SE only, not those at N, S, E, W.

Adding one or more of these features to the study of cellular automata immediately makes the overall population evolution more complex. However, as all cells are not then, strictly speaking, equal, it does mean that pockets of different behaviours can appear. This can easily mean that various different behaviours appear in one overall world, sometimes clashing and affecting each other both temporally and spatially.

TOTALISTIC CELLULAR AUTOMATA

As we have seen in the previous section, from the basic foundation of cellular automata, there are many variations possible. One special case exists when, rather than being 1 or 0, the state of each cell can be represented by a number (usually an integer). In the same sort of way as we have witnessed thus far, the state of each cell at time $t+1$ then depends on some relationship with the state of that cell at time t along with the state of its neighbours. For example, it may be that the new state of the cell at time $t+1$ is simply a summation of the states of the cell and its neighbours at time t, divided by nine – the number of cells being employed.

It is apparent that very quickly totalistic cellular automata can become extremely complicated. Not only can the updating rule for a cell be much more complex – involving mathematical functions of considerable depth – but also some of the variations discussed in the previous section can be brought to bear. This is an area that has, perhaps surprisingly, to this time only been researched to a limited extent and we are yet to discover many patterns and numerical phenomena that could easily exist, some possibly by the use of very straightforward rule extensions.

REVERSIBLE CELLULAR AUTOMATA

A further special case of cellular automata worth looking at is when they are reversible. This is the situation if, for every possible configuration of a cellular automata world at a particular time $(t+1)$, there is one and only one immediately previous configuration (t). These reversible cellular automata are directly useful in studying physical phenomena such as fluid or gas dynamics, an important aspect being that they obey the laws of thermodynamics.

Cellular automata of this type have specific sets of rules which enable the reversibility to occur. The types of rules that achieve this are therefore also a feature of study. Even for very simple, 1/0 types of cellular automata it is not an easy task to prove that only one previous state could have resulted in the present state. Some techniques, such as partitioning the entire world into specific groupings, can bring about such proofs more easily, although in doing so they can change the general definitions applied.

For non-reversible cellular automata, patterns can exist for which there are no previous states. Such patterns are referred to as **Garden of Eden patterns**, because they are patterns which no previous pattern can lead to through the evolution of the world. Garden of Eden patterns can only be realised as start-up arrangements input by the user.

EVOLVING SOFTWARE A-LIFE

As we have seen in the previous section, considerable complexity can arise even from simple beginnings by following simple rules. All that is needed is a world populated by entities of some kind, which are affected not only by themselves but also socially by those around them. With cellular automata the entities were merely squares on a board, which could be in a particular state at any time. It is quite possible, however, for the entities to be more complex and to have something of a biological or real-world link. This is much more difficult to do if we actually want to create the entities in real life; however, within a computer, as simulations, it is possible.

It is not only the case that entities can be simulated but also that they can exist within a virtual world. The world can have its own set of rules, some of which are to do with the state of each of the entities within the world, and hence their evolution, and some are to do with how the entities interact – not something that was apparent with cellular automata. The entities can be based on biological beings, living in a representation of the real world, or they can be purely imaginary, living in an imaginary world.

In particular, different techniques in AI, as discussed thus far, can be applied to the entities in a virtual world, so each entity can make its decisions using a neural network or through a fuzzy expert system. This decision making can itself evolve due to some of the GAs guiding the changes – as long as the decision making can be encoded for the algorithm to use. The added advantage here is that entities can be mixed together to (genetically) form the next generation of entities. For example, the virtual world could be populated by cyclops fish as shown in Figure 5.1. Here, a fish can move around by means of rocket thrusters on its right and left side. It has one eye which has a retina based on an ANN. To survive, the fish needs to learn to recognise food pellets and then to coordinate its thrusters in order to move towards a pellet and eat it.

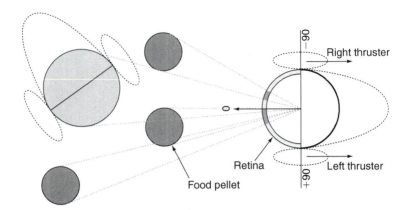

Figure 5.1 Cyclops fish simulation.

This learning can partly be carried out by means of straight-forward AI, but partly it can also be carried out by genetic means – successful cyclops fish 'mating' with other successful cyclops fish in order to produce offspring which form the next generation. The big advantage of computer simulation here is that the time taken to calculate a new generation is very short – in fact, within a few seconds, for a small population, thousands of generations could be investigated. A small change to the initial population and a whole new evolutionary pathway can be investigated very quickly.

Simulated evolution has the big advantage of being extremely fast. As we will see shortly, this technique can also be used to play an important role in developing much-improved hardware, including real-world entities such as robots.

In Figure 5.2 we can see an example of what can occur even with a relatively simple neural network. Here the cyclops fish ANN brain has evolved over 200 generations into quite a complex decision-making mechanism – linking sensory input from the retina to motor thrusters. Hence it has learnt what to do when it can 'see' food in order to move itself towards the food pellets and eventually to capture them.

Even though it only consists of ten neurons, the network is extremely complicated and attempting to figure out exactly how the fish will behave in certain circumstances is by no means a

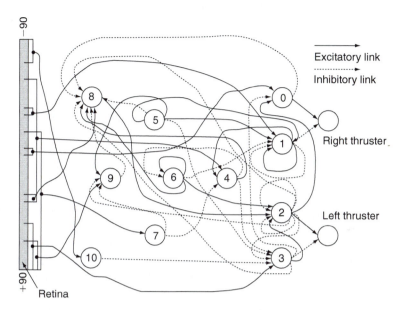

-90

+90

Excitatory link

Inhibitory link

Right thruster

Left thruster

Retina

Figure 5.2 Cyclops fish evolved neural network.

simple task. The network has evolved on a genetic basis, successful traits being strengthened, with failures tending to cause a weakening of connections that brought them about.

Although the sensory input and motor output of each of the fish are identical in software, due to different successes with different food pellets at different times, each fish developed in this way has a slightly different network set-up after 200 generations and therefore the fish behave differently – some perhaps better at their form of life than others. A change in the environment at any time – for example, different sized pellets – may well mean that some of the fish are not as well adapted as before and they may die off, whereas others may become better suited to the changed surroundings.

PREDATOR–PREY CO-EVOLUTION

Rather than evolving software A-life as merely one species, it is interesting to consider virtual worlds in which one species acts as predator while another is its prey. For the predator to be successful, it must catch reasonable prey without expending too much energy. For the prey to be successful it must avoid the predator, again without expending too much energy. However, if the predator is too successful this also causes problems as there will soon be no prey left for it to feed on.

Typical first generations of both predators and prey can exhibit a relatively random behaviour. With the predators trying to get close to the prey and the prey trying to get a good distance from the predators, after just a few generations the predators effectively pursue the prey; however, the prey is also quite effective at evading the predators. So it goes on. If, over the course of several generations, the predators improve considerably, then the less effective prey strategies will quickly die out, leaving the more successful strategies to have more of an impact on future generations.

Essentially, a co-evolution occurs, the evolution of both the predator and prey being dependent on the external environment which, in this case, includes the other species. Any dramatic change in either species could completely destroy the happy balance of the system.

Although what has been described here has been merely two species, this is really just to serve as a simple example. Much more complex virtual worlds are easily constructed with both cooperating species and/or prey which is in turn predator of its own prey.

VIRTUAL WORLDS

A considerable volume of virtual world software is readily available online and it is well worth a search to view different alternatives. For example, you will find 'Gene Pool' in which the swimmers are evolved over generations in terms of colour, length, motion and so on. You will also discover virtual creatures in which software genes are employed to describe both the neural network of each creature as well as its body as a whole. Technological creatures have been evolved for various simple tasks, such as swimming, walking, jumping and following.

Another example is the Golem project in which both the body and brain of technological entities are evolved in terms of designs which are physically accurate representations of real-world artefacts. Concluding designs have then actually been fabricated using a rapid prototype machine – only real motors need to be added. Therefore, an artefact is evolved in a simulation to perform an act, such as moving across a table. The evolved solution in the simulation is then fabricated into a real item and it can perform the movement in the real world.

This feature indicates a distinct advantage of evolution through simulation. If hardware robots or machines were built and evolved through real-world interaction, it could take quite some time before improvement is witnessed. As long as the simulation is reasonably representative of the real world and a robot can also be accurately represented in the simulation, then evolution can occur within the simulation over thousands of generations – possibly merely taking a few real-world seconds – with the final solution being realised by means of a real-world build.

HARDWARE ROBOTS AS A FORM OF A-LIFE

An A-life simulation can be, as we have seen, an extremely powerful tool, particularly due to its advantage of the speed of calculation of each new generation. However, even though it provides a wonderfully flexible test bed for AI algorithms, it is merely a virtual world within the computer with no tangible output unless time is halted while a real-world analogy of an entity within the software is manufactured. In a simulation, entities are 'alive' (in some sense) within the computer, but it is difficult to argue that they are really alive! In the true sense of A-life, what we need are physical entities that exist in the real world.

AI and its relation with sensory input and motor output, particularly in terms of providing the thinking power for a robot, will be investigated in the next chapter. Here, however, a brief look is taken at some of the main issues affecting the realisation of hardware A-life entities by means of a robot base.

SEVEN DWARF ROBOTS

In order to consider some fundamental aspects of A-Life, some simple robots have been constructed, as shown in Figure 5.3, called the seven dwarf robots (mainly because there were seven of them initially built). They have relatively few sensors and move around by means of two independent drive wheels at their rear with a small (non-drive) castor ball-wheel for stability, at their front.

The drive wheels can go forwards or backwards, so the robot can move around and turn quickly. Typically, the forward-only sensors are ultrasonic which means that the robot obtains an indication of objects to its front left, front centre and/or front right as appropriate, as can be seen in Figure 5.3. With a relatively simple mode of operation they provide an ideal platform on which to study some of the principles of A-life.

At any particular time the robot's sensors will provide specific information on the robot's position with regard to other objects. For example, the readings could be: object close front right; object medium distance front centre; no object front left. This is a state of the robot at a certain time. In this case it probably means there is something to the front right of the robot. If the robot continued to move forwards and turn right, then it would likely hit the object. The robot's situation can therefore be categorised in terms of the state it is in – as just described in terms of the sensor readings at a particular time.

In each state the robot has a probability of performing a particular action with its wheels. For example, left wheel forwards fast, right wheel backwards slow, which would cause the robot to spin to the right. When first initialised, all possible such actions have a roughly equal probability of being performed.

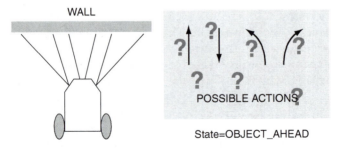

Figure 5.3 Seven dwarf robot.

REINFORCEMENT LEARNING

When any specific action is taken (the robot will of course be in some state) the resulting state situation is examined and categorised as being either 'good' or 'bad'. For actions taken which result in a 'good' state, a positive reinforcement takes place; i.e. the probability of the same action being taken when the robot is in the same situation in the future is increased. For actions which result in a 'bad' state, a negative reinforcement takes place; i.e. the probability of that action being taken when the robot is in the same situation in the future is decreased.

Over time, as the robot moves around and interacts with the environment, so different actions in different situations (different states) are evaluated. If (for example) the robot is given a target goal to move forwards but not to bump into anything, the robot will quickly learn by positive reinforcement that going forward in the open is 'good'. Under repeated reinforcement, suitable wheel movements that achieve this action will develop a very high probability of being taken.

In terms of the state of the robot, this means that when all three of the robot's sensors indicate that there is no object apparent, both wheels will move forward fast as a learned action. Consequently, other possible actions will become very unlikely in this state. The robot will also learn that going forward near a wall is 'bad' due to negative reinforcement. Under repeated reinforcement this action will develop a low probability in this state, meaning other possible actions will be far more likely to be taken.

Each time the robot is switched off and switched back on again its memory is erased. As a result of this, depending on the environment, the robot can exhibit different behaviours at the end of each run. This often depends on what it tries, in a certain state, early on and whether this action results in a good or bad conclusion. As an example, if the first time the robot moved into a corner the attempted action was to spin to the right and this succeeded, then the robot would be more likely to attempt the same action next time – as a result, the action would become even more likely still. So the robot can pick up particular behaviours through a successful sequence of results.

REINFORCEMENT LEARNING: PROBLEMS

Assessing when the robot is being successful and when not can be very difficult to achieve in practice. In the example described it is not particularly problematic – for example, when the robot's sensors indicate the presence of an object, that is a direct measure. If, as a result of an action, an object gets closer (according to the sensor readings) then the action taken was a bad one. In a more complex environment, however, the evaluation of robot behaviour can need much 'tweaking' in order to get it to work correctly. This is especially true when the overall goal of the robot is not (apparently) directly connected to its immediate behavioural action.

In some situations it is not possible to know whether an action is good or bad until some time after a decision event; that is, the reward or punishment may be delayed. For example, consider a robot mouse finding its way through a maze, such as that depicted in Figure 5.4.

Such a robot is slightly more complicated than the seven dwarf robot we have just looked at in that it requires elements of memory and planning to find its way to the end goal. In this case the robot

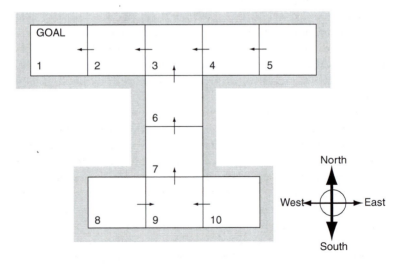

Figure 5.4 Simple robot maze.

mouse receives no reward until it has found its way to the 'cheese' at the end (goal) of the maze. In such cases it is not always possible to use simple reinforcement, as the rewards are delayed.

In our example, each square represents a position or state the robot mouse can be in at any time. The robot is free to move in any of the directions: north, south, east or west from each square. For any start point, the arrows in Figure 5.4 show the optimum/ fastest path to the end/goal state which is square 1. When the robot reaches the goal it obtains a reward.

Many intermediate steps are required to be taken by the robot in order for it to reach the goal, where it receives its reward. The question is: how should correct actions in previous states be rewarded? In this case, for example, if the robot starts from square 8 it is best for it to move in sequence to squares 9, 7, 6, 3, 2 and finally to 1 in order to reach the goal.

TEMPORAL DIFFERENCE ALGORITHMS

In an example such as the maze of Figure 5.4, how best should an overall reward, which is goal driven, be divided amongst the many actions and states that ultimately lead the robot to the goal? A common solution to such problems is to use a **temporal difference algorithm**.

Let us assume that if the robot eventually gets to the end goal it will receive a reward of +100 for arriving at square 1. However, if square 1 is the perfect end point solution then perhaps being in state 2 isn't that bad as it can readily lead to state 1, simply by the robot moving west. So we could assign a reward value for getting to state 2 based on its own reward (if there is one) AND some element of the reward that is expected when it reaches state 1.

In turn, as we now have an updated version of the reward for getting to state 2, we could reason that going west from state 3 might not be so bad and so on. Temporal difference learning allows for such a reward to slowly filter down through a chain of states as exploration proceeds. In the case of the very simple maze considered, it is all relatively straightforward. However, in problems like this parallel or even multiple paths may exist, so one route may be much better/faster than another route. This can be reflected in the rewards assigned at different points throughout the maze.

The overall key element is for the robot mouse to find its way to the goal, even if it takes a round-about route. Once it has found a solution then maybe it can improve on that solution by trying a different route next time it has a go. This can even be seen in Figure 5.4, where the robot could travel east when in state 9 to get to state 10, then travel west from state 10, back to state 9 and then north from state 9 to state 7.

While this is by no means a sequence of moves which fits into the best solution, nevertheless it can result in the robot subsequently arriving at the goal. Filtering down rewards, as in the case of the temporal difference algorithm, must therefore also take into account changing the value of a particular reward over time. Here, we would wish to deter the robot from going the route just described, in which it would unnecessarily take in state 10. We need it to be more attractive to move from state 9 directly to state 7, rather than to 8 or 10.

However, if the robot did (by mistake!) move from state 9 to state 10, we would still wish to encourage it, through reward, to move back to state 9 as quickly as possible. This means punishing a robot for retracing its steps is probably not a good idea – if the robot felt it was not good to move back to 9 from 10 then it might just sit at 10 and never move, so it needs to be encouraged to shift in a good direction.

The complexity of such algorithms can include an overall energy value which depletes with respect to time – simply by moving the robot can pick up energy. This strategy ensures that the robot keeps going. The norm is then for the robot to take several attempts to find the goal – the route with the greatest reward will be the one it subsequently performs in later trials. It can in these cases be best for the robot to try different possibilities at different attempts, such that it might eventually 'stumble' across a better solution. The time taken in searching for a solution, the need for the optimal solution and actual energy expended by the robot are all factors in the practical realisation of this problem.

COLLECTIVE INTELLIGENCE

As we saw from our previous discussion of cellular automata, an overall complex behaviour can emerge from the interaction of relatively simple cellular elements. It could be said that this is the sort of process that goes on in a neural network such as the human brain. It does, however, point to a more general type of intelligence, namely **collective intelligence**. This is the type of group or shared intelligence that emerges from the collaboration and competition of many individuals which are not, in themselves, necessarily simple.

Such intelligence can be observed in animals, especially humans, even bacteria and, importantly, in computer networks. It stems from the concept that seemingly independent individuals can cooperate so closely as to become indistinguishable from a single organism, as is the case of an ant colony, with each ant acting as the cells of a single 'superorganism'. H.G. Wells referred to this phenomena as a 'World Brain'. It can be witnessed regularly in humans and other creatures as group behaviour – even explained by/as mass suggestion.

One everyday appearance of collective intelligence is in the area generally referred to now as **new media.** With this, the ability to store and retrieve information through databases and the internet allows for information to be shared without difficulty. Thus knowledge easily passes between cells (humans). It is a form of networking and high-speed information passing enabled by the internet.

In a sense the collective merger of groups of humans and networked computers allows both the manipulation and use of the knowledge therein for both individual and collective benefit. Overall, however, it is the ability of networked technology to enhance community knowledge and make it readily available that is a powerful tool. Indeed, because of its community basis, knowledge repositories linked into the network take on a group viewpoint (as shown by Wikipedia), rather than the heavily biased perspectives previously exhibited by tools such as encyclopaedias and the like (biased towards the publishers, for example).

One excellent example of this form of AI is the use of collective intelligence to predict stock market prices and their movement. This has become more than just a viable option for human operatives; it has completely taken over from them in many cases. In some cases aggregated current stock market information is presented along with views from both human stock analysts and AI predictions. Human investors can submit their financial opinions, with the end result being that an amalgamated human–machine opinion is created. The opinion of humans and machines can be weighed to reflect a broad spectrum of stock market expertise, which can ultimately be utilised to more accurately predict the behaviour of financial markets.

On the basis of considerable evidence in terms of financial gain, funds of this type have become very popular investment options using the collective intelligence of the market, rather than simply the judgement of professional fund managers, as an investment strategy.

SWARM INTELLIGENCE

A different form of intelligence results from collective or collaborative behaviour when each of the individuals connected into the network are no longer extremely simple elements but rather have at least some limited intellectual abilities. Indeed, it may be that each individual has its own goals and maintenance program that even involves self-organisation. A key point here is that they are a member of a collective and it is (as the name suggests) the operation of the collective that is the critical factor.

In AI systems swarm intelligence has, thus far, been mainly focused on in terms of either hardware, real-world cellular robotic systems or software agents performing a particular task within an overall program. In the case of robots, they are often relatively small in size and of the same type, but this is more for ease of implementation.

Swarm intelligence is typically made up of a population of relatively simple robots or agents interacting locally with one another as well as with their environment. Indeed, depending on the nature of the network connection between them, the environment can be a different one for each of the agents. The agents tend to follow simple rules, and although there is no centralised control structure dictating how individual agents should behave, interactions between such agents lead to the emergence of apparently intelligent, global behaviour, which may well be unknown to the individual agents. A natural example of this phenomenon can be seen in bird flocking.

When employed with robots, such principles are generally referred to as 'swarm robotics', while the term 'swarm intelligence' usually refers to the more general set of procedures employed or decisions taken. 'Swarm prediction', meanwhile, has been used in the specific context of forecasting problems. Biological inspiration is also behind several different optimisation techniques, where an attempt is made to find the best solution to a problem based on a method observed in the biological world. The most popular and successful of these will now be described in general terms.

ANT COLONY OPTIMISATION

By taking inspiration from the function of an ant colony, software methods can be obtained which are useful in problems that need to find paths to goals. Artificial 'ants', in the form of software agents, find optimal solutions to sub-problems by moving through a space which represents all possible solutions. In the real world, ants lay down pheromones, a chemical trail directing each other to resources while exploring their environment.

In a similar fashion the simulated 'ants' record their positions and the quality of their solutions and pass on this information to other 'ants'. As a result, in later iterations more such ants can locate better solutions. A slight variation on this approach is the Bees algorithm, which is analogous to the foraging patterns of the honey bee – nevertheless, much of the same principles apply.

PARTICLE SWARM OPTIMISATION

Particle swarm optimisation (PSO) is a global search and optimisation method for dealing with problems in which the best solution can be represented as a point in multidimensional space. Different hypotheses are first plotted in the space and are seeded with what is referred to as an 'initial velocity', as well as a communication channel between the particles. Particles then move through the solution space and are evaluated according to a fitness criterion.

Over time, particles are accelerated towards those particles within their communication grouping which exhibit better fitness values. The main advantage of such an approach over other global optimisation strategies is that due to the large number of members that make up the particle swarm, the technique is extremely unlikely to be caught up in local minima – a global solution is by far most likely.

STOCHASTIC DIFFUSION SEARCH

Stochastic diffusion search (SDS) is an agent-based global search and optimisation technique best suited to problems where the objective goal can be broken down into independent partial-goals. Each agent maintains its own hypothesis, which is iteratively tested by evaluating a randomly selected partial-goal parameterised by the agent's current hypothesis. In the standard version of SDS such partial evaluations are binary, resulting in each agent becoming either active or inactive.

Information on hypotheses is diffused across the population of agents by means of a one-to-one inter-agent communication strategy which is similar to the technique used by a tandem-running ant to lead another ant from nest to food. A positive feedback mechanism ensures that, over time, a population of agents stabilises as the agents flock around the globally best solution. SDS is both efficient and robust in relation to the problem to be solved.

INTELLIGENT WATER DROPS

This is a swarm-based, nature-inspired optimisation method, which is based on the observed changes in routing of natural rivers and how they find close-to-optimal paths between source and mouth. The end result is at least a reasonable one, even if not exactly optimal. The near-optimal path of a river, at a point in time, follows from actions and reactions which occur both between water droplets and between the water and the riverbed.

In the IWD software procedure, artificial water drops cooperate to change their environment in such a way that the optimal path for the drops, acting as a collective, is eventually revealed. Solutions are incrementally constructed by the IWD algorithm based on a population of water drops.

HYBRID SYSTEMS

In many cases an artificially intelligent system is developed to tackle a specific task, which is a real-world problem. It may well be that the designer has their own particular type of AI that they are well versed in and that they like to use. However, one technique may not provide a good solution to the problem. What is usually wished for is the best possible solution, regardless of the method employed. In many cases it is therefore typical that not just one AI method is employed, but rather an amalgam of several techniques, combined together in a hybrid solution to best tackle the problem in hand.

BIOLOGICAL AI BRAINS

Until recently it has been the case that the whole concept of AI has been associated with its employment on a silicon machine base – a computer system made up of technological elements. In fact, up to now this book has focused on this specific type of AI because historically the philosophy and construct of AI systems has been targeted on that basis.

In Chapter 3 it was seen that most philosophical ideas of consciousness have been rooted largely in the emergent nature of a collective of biological neurons, principally with the aim of distinguishing it from anything apparently emanating from a machine. Recently, however, this boundary has been blurred by the introduction of biological brains, a form of AI realised by growing biological neurons.

While it has for some time been quite possible to culture (grow) biological neurons in a dish, the critical developments of late have involved embodying the culture within a robot body. Essentially, the brain is grown and is given a robot body with which it can sense the world and move around in it. It must be acknowledged that such development is still in its infancy, but already it has a role to play in the field of AI and raises numerous questions with regard to its future development.

As this approach is distinctly different to that considered thus far in this book, here we will first take a look at the basic technique involved and then consider some of the implications as the technology is developed, particularly insofar as they affect the philosophy and deployment of AI systems in general.

CULTURING NEURONS

A cultured brain is created by collecting and separating the neurons found in cortical (biological) brain tissue using enzymes, and then growing them in an incubator, providing suitable environmental conditions and nutrients at a constant temperature (typically 37°C). In order to connect a culture with its robot body, the neurons are grown in a small dish, on the base of which is an array of flat micro electrodes. This provides an electrical interface with the neuronal culture.

Once spread out on the array and fed, the neurons in such cultures spontaneously begin to grow and shoot branches. They connect with nearby neurons and commence both chemical and electrical communication. This propensity to spontaneously connect and communicate demonstrates an innate tendency to network. The neuronal cultures themselves form a layer over the electrode array, effectively growing into a two-dimensional brain.

The electrode array enables output voltages from the brain to be monitored from each of the electrodes and for the brain to be stimulated by the application of appropriate voltage signals. In this way both motor output and sensory input can be achieved. The monitored signals can be employed to drive the motors of a robot body and move the robot around, while sensory signals from the robot body can be used to apply different stimulating, sensory pulses. A feedback loop is formed, incorporating the robot body with its new cultured brain.

Several different schemes have thus far been constructed in order to investigate the ability of such systems. These vary in terms of both the method of applying signals to stimulate the culture (how big, how frequent, etc.) and in terms of how the response of the brain is interpreted (how many electrodes are monitored, whether they are filtered, averaged, etc.). The input–output relationship between the culture and its robot body is a focus of ongoing research as better methods are realised.

PRESENT-DAY EMBODIMENT

Present-day ongoing research usually involves the removal of the neural cortex from the foetus of a rat in order to provide the initial neural culture. The culture must be fed with a drink of minerals and nutrients which are inserted into the culture's dish, which acts as a bath. This bath must be refreshed every two days in order to both provide a food source for the culture and to flush away waste material.

By the time the culture is only one week old, electrical activity can be witnessed to appear relatively structured and pattern forming in what is, by that time, a very densely connected matrix of neurons. Typically, the arrays presently employed consist of an 8×8 or 10×10 array of electrodes measuring approximately $50\,\text{mm} \times 50\,\text{mm}$. Each of the electrodes is approximately 30 micrometres in diameter.

Thus far a modular closed-loop system between a (physical) mobile robotic platform and a cultured neuronal network has been successfully achieved using the electrode array method described, allowing for bidirectional communication between the culture and the robot. It is estimated that presently each culture typically consists of approximately 100,000 densely connected neurons. This can be compared with 100 billion neurons in a typical human brain or a few hundred, or less, in the brain of a slug or snail.

BIOLOGICAL AI BRAIN: CHALLENGES

Apart from generally improving the reliability of an overall robot with a biological brain, several challenges are presently being targeted, not the least of which is getting the robot to learn.

Habitual learning has been recognised; this is the type of learning that occurs when something is done repetitively. A human often says that something becomes automatic or they are performing a task without even thinking about it. In fact, such learning is due to specific neural pathways in the brain being repetitively stimulated, causing the pathways to strengthen until a particular set of sensory signals causes a particular response – effectively, the brain is sort of programmed. By requiring a robot with a biological brain to behave in a particular way – say, avoiding an object when it moves towards it – this type of habitual learning can be witnessed in the brain, the neural pathways physically strengthening.

It is also possible to apply different chemicals to parts of the brain of the robot to either enhance neural development or to restrict neural growth. In this way the robot can (chemically) be made to improve its performance – a different type of learning. Meanwhile, the more standard form of reinforcement learning – rewarding and punishing the robot to get it to improve its behaviour in some way – is presently problematic. Questions being faced are: how do you reward such a robot with electrical or electro-chemical signals? How can such signals be made meaningful to the robot?

Another challenge is the use of human neurons, taken from human embryos, rather than rat neurons. This certainly throws up some technical issues, mainly in terms of development time – while rat neurons tend to develop over a 21–28-day period, human neurons take 18 years or so. While a one-month time span is very useful for laboratory purposes, carrying out an experiment over 18 years can prove rather expensive! The point to be made here, though, is that human neurons can be employed to form a biological brain within a robot body.

Some present research is aimed at providing a small encapsulated, pseudo-incubator that sits on top of a robot. The aim is for the culture to exist within this attempt at a robot head. So instead of growing in a remote incubator, linking up with its robot body through a wireless connection, it may well be possible for the brain to actually travel around on top of its body. At present, however, numerous practical problems exist with this, not the least of which is dealing with the vibrations that are caused when the robot moves around.

A more direct technical challenge is presently to increase the overall size of the culture in terms of the total number of neurons contained. A primary step in this move is a shift towards a three-dimensional growth rather than the two-dimensional method described earlier. Lattice methods are now being researched for just this purpose. While this has the potential to increase the overall power of the brain, it does present a significant problem in understanding what exactly is going on in the central area of the volume.

ROBOT CONSCIOUSNESS

In Chapter 3 we looked at the question of consciousness in a human and the possibility of consciousness in an AI system. Some of the stronger defensive philosophical arguments (particularly those of Searle and Penrose) essentially place the emphasis on the need for the collective operation of human brain cells in order to realise consciousness.

Searle claimed that consciousness emerges from the collective operation of human neurons, while Penrose asserted that no matter how closely we might be able to copy these brain cells with silicon technology, we will always miss out by a little bit, and that is the critically important bit for consciousness to occur in a robot. Essentially, the argument is that because a robot silicon brain is not exactly the same as a human brain, we can conclude that it is not conscious.

In this chapter we have discussed the culture of a biological brain, possibly from human neurons, and its placement within a robot body. The lattice-culturing methods being investigated allow for a three-dimensional brain to be kept alive and embodied, which means we will, before long, have a robot brain with (typically) 30 million neurons. In fact, looking ahead a little, it is not completely out of bounds to speculate on the realisation of a three-dimensional volume brain consisting of over 60 billion neurons – more than half the size of a typical human brain.

So how do we now consider the consciousness of our robot when it has a brain that consists of 60 billion densely packed, highly connected and developed human neurons? Can we endow it with genuine understanding and therefore genuine intelligence? If so, we will definitely have to think about giving the robot voting rights and allowing it to live its own life, whatever that means – possibly even putting it in prison if it does something it shouldn't.

Indeed, it is difficult – based on the philosophical arguments employed thus far – to argue against such a biologically brained robot being conscious. It might be for some that 60 billion is still not 100 billion and that's all there is to it. If so, then maybe we need to start counting the number of brain cells in each human's head such that those whose total falls below a threshold (let's say 80 billion) will find themselves dropped from the human race on the grounds that they are no longer a conscious being!

The point here is that in placing a biological brain (particularly when made up of human neurons) within a robot body, it bridges the gap between the operation of a human brain and that of a computer/machine brain. It also undermines many of the philosophical arguments (as we can see), which conclude some sort of superlative for the human brain. Perhaps it makes us think again, this time a little more deeply, about the differences between robots, AI and humans. Perhaps it also makes us ask more pertinent questions about what being a human actually means.

CONCLUDING REMARKS

In this chapter we have taken a look at embodied AI in terms of robotics. In particular, by considering A-life, we took a look both at life within a computer simulation and actual physical life within a body, moving around in the real world.

As soon as A-life is considered in terms of the existence of an individual, whether that individual exists inside a computer or indeed if the computer exists as a brain inside the individual, then that individual's role within a society becomes important. Fundamental studies on relationships can be carried out by looking at cellular automata – relatively simple entities which interact with other nearby similar entities. It can be seen that even if the entities are basic and the relationships with other entities are relatively trivial, extremely complex social behaviours can apparently emerge. Such results make one reflect on the nature of human society, where the individuals and the relationships are far more complex and much less standardised. This is an area where much further study can be carried out.

The same complexity in interaction is true for other collective robot behaviours, and here we looked briefly at collective intelligence, swarm intelligence and hybrid intelligence – all in terms chiefly of their practical realisation.

The latter part of this chapter is the most novel area of AI at this time – the concept of growing a biological form of AI. In this case, what is described here merely takes a glimpse at future possibilities. As the support technology is developed, so larger cultures will be grown with more sensory input and with more powerful motor outputs. Even in their present form it is impossible to claim that such robots are not alive – particularly in terms of brain life. It is expected that this area of AI will expand dramatically in the years ahead.

KEY TERMS

artificial life, cellular automata, collective intelligence, Garden of Eden patterns, new media, temporal difference algorithm

FURTHER READING

1   *Introduction to Robotics: Mechanics and Control* by J.J. Craig, published by Addison-Wesley, 2004. An in-depth book concerned mainly with the science and engineering of mechanical manipulators.

2   *Supervised Reinforcement Learning: Application to an Embodied Mobile Robot* by K. Conn, published by VDM Verlag, 2007. This book describes experiments involving a real, mobile robot. It considers biological inspiration, navigation and supervised learning.

3   *Collective Intelligence in Action* by S. Alag, published by Manning, 2008. This is a hands-on guidebook for implementing collective intelligence. The emphasis is on the underlying algorithms and technical implementation.

4   *Swarm Intelligence: From Natural to Artificial Systems* by E. Bonabeau, M. Dorigo and G. Theraulaz, published by Oxford University Press, 1999. This book contains a detailed look at models of social insect behaviour and how to apply these models in the design of robots and complex systems.

5   *Computing with Instinct*, edited by Y. Cai, published by Springer-Verlag, 2011. This is a collection of essays by experts on topics pertinent to AI in robotics and the future. In particular, it contains more in-depth material on biological AI.

6

SENSING THE WORLD

SYNOPSIS

When considering intelligence it is worth remembering that a large proportion of the human brain is devoted to sensory input. In insect brains the proportion is even greater – often exceeding 90% of the total operational cells. Sensing the world therefore has a huge impact on intelligence. Without input how can an entity perceive the world, respond, learn or communicate? The nature of the sensory input dictates the nature of the entity. In this chapter we consider how sensory input is dealt with in machine systems. We look here at the processes involved in computer vision and other sensing systems such as audio, ultrasonics, infrared and radar.

VISION

As far as human brains are concerned, by far the overriding sensory input is that of vision. The nature of human visual input, by means of stereo (two eyes) sight near the top of our bodies, which can be rotated and scanned, is often regarded as the single most important aspect of the human success story on Earth. That, of course, and the associated brain development that has gone along with it. Some scientists even estimate that two-thirds of the neurons in the human brain are devoted entirely to dealing with visual input.

If machines are to operate in a world which has been constructed by human ingenuity, largely for human use, then it seems sensible that vision systems which form part of an AI system are capable of a similar performance when dealing with viewing the world and understanding what is seen. It has to be said that although much research has gone into developing computer vision systems, by far the bulk of work in the design of AI has been focused on central problem solving, planning and decision-making aspects rather than sensory signal processing. Also, as we saw in Chapter 3 when looking at the philosophy of AI, this has concentrated more on abstract internal issues such as consciousness rather than arguably more important topics such as how AI comprehends what it is looking at.

Partly because of technological developments in terms of cameras (television and charge coupled devices – CCDs), AI vision is a relatively new field of study. In the early days of computing, it was difficult to process large sets of image data. However, as cameras became much smaller, cheaper and robust, and hardware memory became more powerful and cost-effective, in the 1970s and 1980s a stronger research effort was targeted in the field.

Interestingly, there is not a well-focused directive for the techniques to apply; rather, there is an abundance of specialised methods for solving well-defined computer vision problems. Each method is often task-specific and can seldom be generalised over a wide body of applications. Many of the methods and applications are, at this time, still in the research arena. However, several methods have found their way into the commercial sector, either as one solution to a particular problem or as part of a library of techniques in a larger system aimed at solving complex tasks such as medical imaging or industrial processes. Usually, in practical computer vision applications, the computers are previously programmed to deal with a particular task, although methods that incorporate some aspects of learning are also becoming quite common.

In this chapter we will take a look at the different elements involved in a computer-based vision system. At this point the discussion will be focused on light acquisition techniques – machine-based versions of the human eye. Other sensory signals which can aid visual understanding, such as radar and range sensors, are dealt with in their own right, separately, later in the chapter.

There are three main elements to dealing with a visual image: first, image acquisition and transformation; second, image analysis; and third, image understanding. Here we take a look at each of these in turn.

IMAGE TRANSFORMATION

Image acquisition and transformation in AI involves converting light images into processed electrical signals that can be used by a computer. This is generally performed by a camera of some type. In fact, the camera is merely replacing the human eye in carrying out the same sort of treatment towards photons of light, and so it is worthwhile briefly looking at how an eye works for comparative purposes.

Light energy enters the eye via the transparent cornea, where it is directed through the pupil. The iris controls the amount of light entering by increasing or decreasing the size of the pupil. The lens then focuses the energy onto the retina. The retina consists of cells called rods (which deal with brightness) and cones (which deal with colour). It is here that an external image, represented by photons of light, in terms of different energy levels, is converted into electrochemical signals which are transported to the brain along the optic nerve. The principle of operation of a camera is very similar to this.

The vast majority of cameras employed with robots nowadays are based on CCD arrays. The reasons for this are that they are small and lightweight, consume little power and are very sensitive. They are made up of an array of small transistors called MOSFETs (metal oxide semiconductor field effect transistors). In these arrays, cells operate rather like individual electric charge-storing capacitors. Light photons pass through a lens and then strike the array, resulting in different positive charges across the array, each charge being directly proportional to the light intensity at that point in the image.

The overall image is, in this way, recorded in the array at a specific time in terms of the different charges across the array. These charges are then transferred (coupled) from one cell to the next by switching the cells positively/negatively, such that the light image is ultimately transferred into an image (frame) buffer as an array of charges. The frame array stores the image temporarily until it is collected and stored by the computer. Typical common CCD arrays consist of 400×500 cells.

IMAGE PIXELS

At a specific time the frame array contains analogue signal elements which are proportional to the light energy across the image. In order for the computer to deal with the image, each analogue element needs to be converted into a digital value. Once in digital form each of the values is referred to as a pixel. If we consider merely a black and white image in the first instance, then typically each pixel will be converted by either an 8-bit or 16-bit analogue-to-digital converter.

Hence, for an 8-bit converter, a perfectly white pixel would become 0 (actually binary 00000000), whereas a perfectly black pixel would become 256 (actually binary 11111111). Different shades of grey are thus represented by all codes in between – converted values are therefore referred to as **grey level** values. A pixel of value 200 would be quite dark; one of 40 would be quite light.

For an image frame array at a particular time, the values stored are converted into a matrix referred to as a **picture matrix**, which is essentially a matrix of greyscale values representative of the image viewed at that instant. To give a typical idea of speed, it may well be that 50 complete frames in a camera are being converted every second, although this figure can be higher if required. However, in some applications – some video games, for example – frame rates of six per second have proven to be sufficiently fast.

Colour images are merely made up of three times what has been described. Effectively, using filters, separate red, green and blue image frames can be obtained and dealt with separately, being mixed together again as required. Many computer vision systems do not deal with colour (and some deal with it only trivially), and hence this facility is not always required. However, if understanding of an image does depend on an analysis of colour values then this can be carried out in terms of the basic red, green and blue constituent components.

IMAGE ANALYSIS

Having obtained a picture matrix which is representative of the external scene being viewed by the camera, the next stage is a requirement to analyse the image. Here the aim is merely to give a basic idea of what is involved.

Image analysis is all about trying to extract meaningful information from the image frames obtained thus far, remembering that now we have digital/binary values that can be operated on by the computer. A task may be very simple, such as reading a barcode tag, or it could be as complex as identifying an individual from a picture of their face. Here we will look at a few fairly general tools that may (or may not) be applicable to a particular problem.

What we are trying to do at this stage of the process is to obtain characteristic information that can ultimately be recognised as being part of an image. Our start point is merely an array of numbers. It is worth remembering that we may be dealing with an array of 400×500 numbers that are arriving (and need to be dealt with in their entirety) 50 times per second. So, in carrying out such an analysis one would tend to look for relatively simple rapid solutions. If time is not a problem, in an offline situation, then clearly more sophisticated techniques may well be possible.

Because the human visual cortex is very good at dealing with vision, ideas about its operation have been taken on board for analysing images. As an example, we considered neural networks in Chapter 4. Different versions of these can be particularly useful in this respect – the N-tuple network being able to deal readily with the required 50 frames per second processing speed.

However, it may be that we consider building fundamental images from the digital greyscale numbers we have to start with, using a sort of line drawing caricature of the image content. In order to build such a picture we need to first extract information on where the lines and edges are in our picture matrix, which is to turn the numerical representation of the matrix into a more graphical, pictorial version.

PRE-PROCESSING

Noise can affect the image in a number of ways (noise being any unwanted signal), particularly because of changes in light intensity over time. What we don't want is to waste time searching for lines and edges in an image only to find that they are not lines at all, but merely distortions due to changing light patterns – importantly, these will shift over time, so they can be filtered out by pre-processing the matrix values before looking for edges.

The simplest form of filtering in one frame is **local averaging**, wherein the value of a pixel is replaced by the average value of that pixel and its neighbours. This considerably reduces the effect of noise in a frame, although it does tend to blur what could otherwise be crisp edges. Consider a section of the picture matrix containing nine greyscale elements:

```
9  7  6
9  8  5
4  4  2
```

In this case the central pixel value 8 is replaced by the average of all the nine values shown – the value 6 in this case. Merely considering the central value, this section of the matrix would become:

```
9  7  6
9  6  5
4  4  2
```

However, apart from the edge values in the overall picture matrix, this procedure would need to be done across the whole image, working systematically. This can be extremely time consuming and in time-critical situations it may well simply be out of the question.

Another form of pre-processing is an attempt to remove what is called salt-and-pepper noise, which amounts to odd changes in the picture matrix that only last for one or two frames and are then gone – maybe due to a conversion error or a brief glint of light. The technique used here is **ensemble averaging**.

In this case the same pixel is viewed over a window of several time steps, essentially four or five versions of the same pixel. An average value is taken over these different versions of the same pixel, so any pixel value changes merely due to salt-and-pepper noise are averaged out.

Once again, this can greatly increase the computational effort and hence the time taken to process an image, especially if many pixels are filtered in this way over many time steps. For both local and ensemble averaging it is best therefore to consider employing such techniques only if they appear necessary given the problem domain.

IMAGE SPECTRUM

It really does depend very much on what the robot could possibly be looking for as to what happens next. Almost surely the robot must focus its attention on a particular spectrum of possible objects in the picture. For example, if the robot is looking for a ball then it is best to focus the image analysis on looking for round objects with a relatively uniform distribution in the shape of a circle.

But even if there are only a relatively small number of potential objects to encounter, their outlines may well be complex. For example, a robot vehicle may need to spot humans, other vehicles, trees, road signs and so on. Each of these shapes is fairly distinct but, depending on the robot's distance from the object, the sizes could be quite different.

FINDING EDGES

As a general approach, unless only one specific object is being searched for, once any apparent noise has been filtered out the next step is to look for any edges or lines in the picture matrix. Ultimately, any edges detected can then be joined together to form a rough outline (a sort of caricature) of an object, which can be compared with a spectrum of shape and object possibilities such that a decision can be made as to what and where the object is. Obviously, other information − such as speed of movement or colour − can be employed to assist in narrowing down the search. Here we look briefly at how to find edges in an image, if these are required.

The characteristic of an ideal edge is a distinct change in pixel value over a very short distance. If the image is scanned, what we are looking for is a large step change in value from one pixel to the next − if this occurs then it is likely that that point is on a line which forms an edge. But for any given image, an edge could appear at any angle, dependent on the orientation of the object. So the step change needs to be checked in all directions.

For this we can use **pixel differentiation**, which simply checks for large changes in pixel magnitude from one pixel to the next, in all directions. Several versions of pixel differentiation exist; a straightforward indicator is shown here for example purposes – called the Roberts Cross Operator. Alternatives can be far more complex. It is found as follows:

A   B
C   D

A, B, C and D are values of four pixels next to each other in the picture matrix. First, we calculate $(A-D)$ and square the answer, then calculate $(B-C)$ and square the answer. The two results are added together and the square root of the total is found. A large final answer indicates that that point is likely to be part of an edge; a small answer indicates that it is unlikely to be part of an edge.

In theory the whole image needs to be scanned at each time step such that all pixels are taken into account. In practice, once an object has first been identified it may only be pixels around where the object is expected to be that need to be used on each scan, although this does depend on how fast an object is likely to be moving, which direction it is moving in and whether the robot is likely itself to be moving to or from the object (hence whether the object is getting bigger or smaller).

At a particular instant in time, for a picture frame, we now have a set of differentiated values. Next, these values are thresholded to decide if they are an edge candidate or not. What this means is that each value from the differentiator is compared with a previously selected threshold value. If it is above the value then it is replaced by a 1, meaning it is an edge candidate, whereas if it is below the value it is replaced by a 0, meaning it is not an edge candidate.

The threshold value may well depend on ambient lighting and the clarity in definition of objects – square-type, sharp objects in strong light may well have crisp edges, whereas squidgy, soft objects in fuzzy light may well have indistinct edges. Nevertheless, it is generally the case that the higher the threshold value is, the fewer edge candidate points there will be; a low threshold value will of course realise a lot of edge points.

Looking at the small example output from a pixel differentiator,

3	41	126	18
38	162	57	23
147	29	17	5
31	10	6	2

we can see that a threshold value of 100 applied to this would produce a binary output image of:

0	0	1	0
0	1	0	0
1	0	0	0
0	0	0	0

which shows a crisp diagonal line of 1s, depicting the partial edge of an object, whereas threshold values of 9 or 200, respectively, would produce binary output images of:

0	1	1	1		0	0	0	0
1	1	1	0	and	0	0	0	0
1	1	1	0		0	0	0	0
1	1	0	0		0	0	0	0

At best, you might say that the left-hand image (relating to a threshold value of 9) depicts a very thick edge, whereas in the right-hand image (relating to a threshold value of 200) the edge has gone altogether.

FINDING LINES

Once a collection of potential edge points have been obtained, these need to be joined together in some fashion in order to decide on what sort of objects are being looked at. To this point in the process the procedures for image capture and processing have been relatively straightforward. Once clear lines have been obtained it can again be a direct process to decide whether it is object A or B that is in front of the robot and where exactly the object is. So, in many ways, accurately finding lines is the most difficult yet important part of a robot's visual portfolio.

What is expected to be in the robot's view can be a main driver at this point in the analysis. The approaches discussed here are therefore merely aimed at presenting the general ideas behind finding lines; the actual approach taken will largely depend on the situation and the spectrum of objects expected. If an object comes into view in general, it will ultimately either be regarded as being like a type of object in memory (e.g. it is a human or tree or vehicle) or it will simply be ignored as being spurious. Learning to recognise completely new objects is an extremely interesting task, but one that is well beyond the scope of the simple tools we consider here.

TEMPLATE MATCHING

A bank of line and object shape templates (a mask) can be stored in memory (e.g. a circle of 1s to represent a ball). A template can then be passed across an image frame to see if it fits any shape of 1s that are apparent. A match is made when a number of 1s in the frame matches those in the template – the actual number chosen to be necessary for it to be considered a good fit depends on the size of the template and the total number of 1s it contains.

This approach can be extremely time-consuming, even to simply pass one template across one frame of the entire image, particularly if this needs to be done every time a new frame arrives, which may well be the case for a moving object. If several templates need to be separately trialled, the time taken can rocket and this can restrict its use if the robot needs to move around and make decisions in real time in the presence of many possible objects – unless large quantities of computing power can deal with it.

It also presents a problem if the robot is moving in relation to the object in view, in that the apparent size and shape of the object may well vary over a relatively short time, requiring a versatile, adaptive template.

However, once an object has been initially spotted it is then possible, from frame to frame over time, to merely inspect the region in the image where the object is roughly expected to be – indeed, this can also take into account changes in size and shape to a large extent. In this way several objects in view can be tracked over time, so it really becomes a case of applying background prior knowledge to the task rather than simply inspecting each frame afresh. The technique can thus also allow for directional movement of the robot and likely directional movement of the object, based on knowledge about the object and its likely pattern of movement.

It may be that rather than an entire object shape being templated, simply a specific arc or region of the outline is considered. The process then is referred to as **model matching** or **pattern matching**. It works by fitting several edges to different models so the overall object picture can be built up. This procedure is useful when information about the size or alignment of the object within the image frame is lacking.

POINT TRACKING

As its name suggests, the method of **point tracking** is extremely basic; in essence, any prior knowledge about the object is largely ignored. Quite simply, the image frame is scanned in a disciplined manner and when a 1 is encountered all neighbouring (not previously scanned) pixels are inspected. If a further 1 or 1s are discovered, these are joined together with the original and the local area around each of the new 1s is inspected. This process is repeated until no further 1s are found – the search then moves on to another region of the image.

This procedure does have a number of advantages. For example, lines do not have to be of a specific thickness which, due to lighting and shadows, is invariably the case in reality – one-pixel-wide perfectly straight lines of 1s in an image are indeed a rarity. Lines also do not have to be a specific shape – straight or circular – which can be particularly useful if we are not sure what angle a robot may approach the viewed object from.

In a practical scanning situation, due to imperfect lines, there may be odd pixels missing. This may appear when two or three separate lines are initially discovered – these lines can be joined together by bridging the gaps. However, it may take further analysis to decide if they are in fact lines belonging to outlines of different objects. Hence different possible outcomes may need to be stored until further details materialise.

It can also be the case that as part of the procedure, when a 1 is encountered, rather than inspecting the immediately neighbouring pixels, a two- or even three-pixel-wide search can be carried out – although clearly there may be time constraints with this. The problem of bridging a gap as opposed to potential separate objects still needs to be resolved, however.

In scanning an image, odd 1s may be encountered that either do not link at all with any other 1s or only link up with a small number of local 1s in an unexpected way. The simplest way of dealing with such instances is to regard these as noise to be ignored.

It could be that a small group of 1s in fact indicates the presence of a tiny and/or distant object in the line of vision. It may well be best to ignore this, even though it is not, strictly speaking, noise – simply because either the object is not relevant to the robot's task in hand or it does not need to be dealt with directly.

However, when a group of 1s is located near a previously detected line, it may be an indication that the line needs to be longer. Both heuristics and (in some form) statistics, particularly involving prediction and comparison with a knowledge base, need to be employed as part of a good vision system.

THRESHOLD VARIATION

One possibility when there are either missing 1s or there exists a small, unconnected group of 1s is to change the threshold value of the specific pixels concerned. For missing 1s, a slight lowering of the threshold may cause these 1s to appear, whereas for unexpected 1s, by slightly increasing the threshold value these 1s may well disappear – in either case this would give more information on the nature of the pixels at the points of interest.

The same routine of threshold variation can also be attempted in the region directly around the pixels of attention. Such an analysis can either confirm that any 1s do potentially link to a previously discovered line or conversely that a line is perhaps not as long as was previously thought. It is worth remembering that the original selection of threshold value is a fairly ad hoc, yet extremely critical, choice and that small variations in the threshold value can severely alter the nature of the image revealed.

SEGMENT ANALYSIS

In many ways the approach to segment analysis is the opposite to that of edge detection in that rather than looking for differences between pixels, the aim is to look for similarities. A located segment or region of the image can then be bordered by an edge, which can be confirmed, if desired, by means of the techniques just discussed.

Although the greyscale value (probably not thresholded) of pixels is one of the factors in shaping out a segment, other aspects such as colour may well help to finalise the analysis. A segment can then signify a specific area of the image which relates directly to an object, such as a person, vehicle or building. The segment can have a well-defined shape and size which is defined by the type and nature of the object in question.

Characteristics and likely performance of that segment can then be linked directly to those of the object. Hence, if it is a building it is not likely to move from one image frame to the next, whereas if it is a vehicle it is likely to move at a particular speed which can be associated with that vehicle under certain conditions.

The big advantage of region analysis is that once a particular region has been identified it is relatively straightforward (and therefore fast) to locate the same region in subsequent image frames. It is also possible to study its relationship with other regions and hence to predict future scenarios – follow on image frames can then be compared with their predicted, or rather expected, behaviour.

FORMING SEGMENTS

Segments can be formed in an image either by **splitting** or **growing**. In splitting, an image is first broken up into areas with similar pixel values – this can be achieved by banding the greyscale values into ranges such as 0–50, 50–100 and so on, then investigating where there are regions of pixels within a certain band. Each region that is so formed can then itself be subdivided into smaller regions on the same basis following tighter bands, until segments are formed exhibiting little variation in greyscale value within them. It may well be that certain of these smaller segments are linked together again – rather like Lego bricks, in the analysis that follows.

In the method of segment growing, the opposite approach is taken in that tight pixel value bounds are started with and from these very small **atomic segments** are formed. These may well each consist of just a small handful of pixels. The process continues by selecting one atomic segment and investigating its neighbouring segments. Where the next segment is similar or is linked by means of prior information – possibly constituent segments of an overall object – these segments can be merged. The neighbouring segments to the merged area are then investigated and further merging may occur. This continues, building up into a final object.

In both segment splitting and segment growing, heuristics are employed extensively to dictate the size of the bands used, the minimum pixel groupings for atomic segments, the segments expected in forming an overall object (which itself can subsequently be a big segment) and so on.

COLOUR

Colour can be used to help detect edges and segments as well as providing an assist in the identification of objects. For AI it is rarely a main line of attack, however. Rather, it adds one more piece of information in helping to understand an image.

With the human eye, it appears that to interpret a colour the human brain integrates the three colour signals (red, blue and green) into a blended whole.

A colour camera indicates signals which relate to the amount of red, blue and green in an image – each pixel being depicted by three separate values. If it is required, an overall colour value for each pixel can be obtained by combining (adding together) the three terms by means of a simple colour equation.

It follows, therefore, that all of the image analysis described thus far for black and white images can be carried out three-fold for the red, green and blue values and/or for overall colour values.

What is particularly useful is the use of colour to indicate uniform areas in terms of the segmentation which has just been described. Analysis of an image can then be further assisted by the use of colour to identify objects, although this has limited application in practice. If a tank is attacking you, deciding whether it is pink or apricot is not as important as deciding that it is a tank.

IMAGE UNDERSTANDING

Image understanding is perhaps the most complex aspect of visual sensory input. Indeed, it is usual for visual information to be combined with other sensory input, which we will shortly look at, to get an overall understanding of what is being viewed. As was just pointed out, colour can sometimes assist in the overall process, as can heuristic knowledge (i.e. what we are expecting to see); the main problem is trying to make sense of the object outlined. A lot of computational effort can be employed on this task alone – indeed, such is the case with human intelligence.

It is worth stating here that many books have been written on this subject alone. The intention here is merely to take a very brief look at what is involved.

If the potential scenarios are fairly well known then it may simply be a case of deciding which one of a small number of potential objects is being viewed. The aim in this case is to compare the image as it stands with a small number of possibilities and see which of these fits most closely. It may be that specific information about likely objects can be used for a simple comparison – a particular shape or size, for instance. However, if a more general understanding is necessary we need to look a little deeper.

BLOCKS WORLD

Up to now we have obtained an image in terms of lines – a sort of caricature. All sorts of shape profiles can then be constructed from these lines, the actual features most likely being dependent on the potential scenario being viewed. One of the simplest approaches in general is to assume that all lines must be straight (no curves) and the world being viewed consists merely of block-shaped objects – a sort of Toytown view of the world.

If lines exist in the image, to be part of an object they must link up with other lines. The first task is therefore to put aside lines that do not link up and focus on lines that link together to form solid objects. The next decision is then about which lines are boundary lines – outlining an object – and which are internal lines depicting convex (sticking out) or concave (leaning in) object features. Such decisions can be taken for all the lines in view in turn, and a number of block-shaped objects will result.

Further decisions then need to be taken as to whether one object is resting on another object or if it casts a shadow over another object and so on, i.e. giving an idea of the relationship between one object and another.

MOVEMENT

It is often the case that either the AI/camera system is attached to a moving vehicle, possibly a robot, or that some of the objects in view will be travelling in a different direction and/or at a different speed. In most cases, therefore, an object in view will move in the image, relative to the AI system. Once an object has been selected it can be segmented in the subsequent images that appear later and tracked from image to image with regard to time.

In a way, this makes subsequent image analysis easier as the object can be looked for in the vicinity of where it appeared in the previous images, taking into account any direction or pattern of movement. This has the added advantage that even if a particular image is badly affected by light or the object is occluded/hidden, the actual shape and identity of the object will already be known – it does not have to be regarded as an unknown object.

Detecting movement is not as easy as it may first appear. What it requires is to find corresponding points, regions and possibly even pixels from one image frame to another. Identifying and subsequently segmenting an object makes this process a lot easier.

TRIANGULATION

Cameras can also be employed to give a reasonably accurate idea of the distance to an object. This can be performed simply by means of stereo vision through the use of two adjacent cameras, as would be the case if they were positioned rather like eyes in a head. If both cameras are then looking at the same object and the angle between each camera and the object can be either measured or calculated – which can be simply found from the position of the object in the two images – then the distance to the object can be calculated by the sine rule which applies to triangles. This is referred to as **triangulation**.

The only other piece of information necessary before an accurate calculation of the distance to the object can be made is the distance between the cameras, which usually would be known precisely. Where two cameras are used, as described, this is referred to as **passive triangulation**. The main problem with this technique is in establishing the exact position of a specific point on the object as it appears separately in the two camera images, something which needs to be found accurately. This is referred to as the **correspondence problem**.

The correspondence problem exists because we need to match a specific point in the image of the object from one camera with the same point in the object's image in the second camera. This is difficult as it cannot be guaranteed that pixels with a particular greyscale value in one image correspond to pixels with the same greyscale value in the second image. The problem is often worsened due to the difference in light intensity between the two cameras.

ACTIVE TRIANGULATION

One way around the correspondence problem is to replace one camera with an active source such as a laser projector. A laser spot is then projected onto the object and the remaining camera can be employed to clearly pick out this spot in the image. The triangulation method can then be used in a similar way to calculate the distance to the object. The known distance between the laser and the camera is very small (a fraction of a foot) in relation to the distance to the object (many feet).

LASERS

Lasers can also be used on their own (without cameras) in order to accurately find the distance to an object. In this case the system emits a short burst of light and measures the time it takes for the light to be reflected off an object and return. As the speed of light is known, simply dividing the total out-and-back time in half indicates the distance to the object. Other aspects of the returning waveform (such as the phase) can also be employed both to simplify the measurement process and to indicate the amount of light absorbed by the object.

It is often the case that a laser can be used to rapidly scan the path ahead in order to get an indication of the distance to objects in the foreground – a sort of laser image. A laser has a very narrow beam width and hence quite an accurate indication of the distance to foreground objects can be obtained, even helping to identify what the objects are from their laser image. This type of system is particularly useful for larger mobile vehicles driving around externally.

SONAR

For closer indications of the distance to objects, especially within buildings, sonar (ultrasound) is often a better option. Indeed, this is the technique used by bats to obtain an accurate picture of distance. On top of this, sonar sensors are relatively cheap, robust and small, and so are ideal for laboratory-scale AI-based robots. Ultrasound also travels at a much lower velocity than light, which means that it is far easier to obtain an accurate measurement of distance. On the negative side, however, the beam width is quite broad. Sonar is therefore not so good at discerning what objects are, but is very good at indicating if there is an object there or not.

Ultrasonics can be used for objects up to 50 feet away, but it works better over just a few feet at most. The procedure requires several pulses of high-frequency sound to be transmitted (usually around twice the highest frequency that the human ear can discern, which is 20 kHz, so a value of 40 kHz can be used), and a calculation is made of the time taken for the signal to travel out and return. As the speed of sound is well known, the distance to an object can be accurately found by dividing the total time in half. If the signal does not return, then there is deemed to be no object present – care does have to be taken in some instances, however, as the signal can sometimes bounce off an object at a strange angle or even be absorbed by an object to some degree.

On the negative side, the signal can be disrupted by other higher frequency sounds, such as jangling keys! Nevertheless, it is relatively easy to operate such sensors and difficult to break them! Usually they are purchased in pairs (sometimes packaged together) with one element transmitting the signal and the second element receiving the reflected signal.

RADAR

Electro-magnetic measurement of distance employs radio signals. This is called radar. The basic principle is the same as that described for both laser and sonar – a radio signal is transmitted and if an object is present the signal is reflected back. The distance to the object can then be calculated by dividing the total out-and-back time in half.

Radar is particularly good at detecting the distance to highly reflective metallic objects and not so good (but by no means out of the question) for non-metallic objects over short distances. Unfortunately, many objects are good at absorbing radio signals, which means that high power is required to increase the strength of the signal. On top of this, a fairly large antenna is usually needed to focus the signal into a narrow beam width. On the positive side, once operative the signal is not so easily disrupted.

Although radar has not been employed for AI-based robotic systems to any great extent in the past, some smaller, reliable units are now available at relatively low cost, making it a viable alternative for some particular applications.

MAGNETIC SENSORS

Rather than giving an indication of the distance to an object, magnetic sensors such as **reed switches** can be used to detect objects that are in close proximity. The switch consists of two magnetic contacts in a small tube. When a magnetic field is nearby (possibly due to the presence of a magnet) the contacts close together, thereby completing an electrical circuit.

Although single switches can be used quite simply to detect the presence or absence of an object, it is more usual for an object to have a magnet attached or to be part of it. As the object moves past several switches so the switches close and open in turn, giving an idea of the speed of the object as it passes by. This technique can be employed for a variety of purposes.

MICRO SWITCH

There are a number of tools a machine can use to detect that something else is nearby. Perhaps the simplest of these is a mechanical switch that operates when it comes into contact with an object. Such switches are relatively cheap, generally robust, simple to arrange and passive, in that, unlike laser beams and even sonar, they do not give away the presence of the robot. This is a positive point for military systems in particular.

Such switches can be placed on various parts of a robot that are likely to come into contact with other objects. When the switch is pressed a simple decision can be taken. Such switches are very useful as a safety feature for factory robots. The switches are linked to the robot's bumpers so that when the bumper comes into contact with an object, a human maybe, a decision such as 'stop moving' can be immediately made. For certain types of military machines, the decision may be to self-explode when the switch is operated – a mine for example.

PROXIMITY SENSORS

One problem with micro switches is that actual contact with an object must be made for the switch to operate and hence for a decision to be made. One advantage of this is that it works with any object – the object to be detected does not have to be modified in any way. Magnetic switches are one alternative for close measurement, but this technique does require magnets to be positioned in or on the objects to be detected.

The same problem is true for other methods that can be used for close proximity measurement, such as inductive or capacitive approaches. For example, in the capacitive technique, one plate of the capacitor must be positioned on the robot and the other plate on a specific object – the electrical capacitance between the plates varies dependent on their distance apart. As an object comes close to the robot so the measured capacitance indicates this. Importantly, the robot and the object do not need to touch each other.

RADIO FREQUENCY IDENTIFICATION DEVICE

Perhaps one of the most widely used proximity sensing methods nowadays is the technique employing a **radio frequency identification device**, commonly referred to as an RFID. It is based on the mutual induction between two coils of wire – one in the RFID and one in a stimulating transmitter. The RFID itself can be in the form of a smart card or a small tube that can be implanted in an object – either biological or technological.

The stimulating transmitter has electrical power connected to it. When the RFID is in close proximity, electrical current is induced in the coil within the RFID by means of a radio frequency signal. This power is merely used to transmit a previously programmed identifying code back to the original stimulating transmitter, which can be connected to a computer. In this way the computer is aware when a specific object carrying a particular RFID is nearby.

This is the basis for identifying tags used in many pets (pet passports), for which the transmitter and RFID need to be within a few inches for sufficient power to be transmitted. The RFID can be the size of a grain of rice for this to work well. Transmitters can also be positioned throughout a building (e.g. in door frames) such that as RFID-carrying entities move around a (computer-integrated) building, so the computer will receive information on where the entity is at any time and hence can respond appropriately. This technique can be used for building security, doors being opened or closed depending on the clearance of an individual or object. In this case the RFID needs to be much larger, typically an inch long or in the form of a smart card. It may be that it is used to indicate objects passing a specific point – to sound an alarm if an item is being stolen from a shop. But the most exciting use is for 'intelligent' buildings, where a computer operates a building's infrastructure depending on RFID information – possibly opening doors, switching on lights and even communicating with individuals, depending on where they are, which way they are heading and so on.

TOUCH

Technology is rapidly being developed either to create (humanlike) hands for robots or as replacement hands for human amputees. The mechanical design of such hands is obviously important, along with their gripping abilities, but so too is the sensory feedback that can be obtained. Micro switches in the fingers are perhaps the easiest method, simply detecting whether or not an object is being touched.

It is possible to arrange a small grid of micro switches in a pad to get an indication of the shape of the object being touched – or at least how a particular object is being touched – depending on which of the switches is operated. Conversely, rather than use a simple on/off switch it is quite possible, through a force sensor, to obtain an indication of how much force is being applied by a finger when it is touching an object. This can be very useful in indicating how much force is necessary if a robot hand needs to maintain a grip.

Other techniques can be used to indicate slippage, and hence that perhaps more force needs to be applied so an object is not dropped. One method involves a type of roller in the finger – as an object slips so the roller rotates. Another approach employs a small microphone – object slippage causes an audio signal to be fed back, with the degree of loudness indicating the amount of slip.

MATERIAL FOR TOUCH

For a particular application it may be that the material coming into contact with an object is not of immediate importance – possibly only a simple switch is involved. However, for general touch-sensing the type of material employed is critical. For example, it usually needs to be very sensitive and respond quickly, yet needs to be robust and deal with different temperatures. Conductive rubber is one type of material that is fairly versatile, but this area is definitely one where ongoing research is critical.

FORCE SENSING

It is also possible to obtain a concept of the force being applied to an object indirectly by measuring the effect of the force on an arm joint or wrist. The most common means of such a measurement is the use of a **strain gauge**. A strain gauge is an extremely reliable, robust and relatively low-cost device that is fairly easy to connect and operate. It gives information on the three rotational forces that can be applied – pitch, roll and yaw.

A strain gauge is essentially a wound length of resistance wire. As its length changes due to a force being applied, so the change in resistance, which is proportional to the length change, can be directly measured. Although the gauge is very sensitive, unfortunately it is also affected by even slight changes in temperature.

OPTICAL SENSORS

Optical sensors tend to be employed for measuring the distance moved by such things as robot joints or wheels. The main principle is that an optical encoder – a set of alternative transparent and opaque stripes – makes use of light detected by a phototransistor. The system generates a series of pulses as the optical encoder, which is directly connected to a robot arm, moves between the light source and the phototransistor, thereby giving an indication of the robot's movement.

The optical encoder can be linear (essentially a flat package) or angular (a disc). The same type of circuit can be used for proximity sensing, in which case it detects when an object enters or exits the beam of light. An infrared light source and phototransistor can be purchased in a single package, with the phototransistor on one side of a slot and the infrared light source on the other side. This is called an optical interrupter.

INFRARED DETECTORS

Infrared detectors are extremely powerful sensing devices in their own right; they detect infrared radiation. Infrared is basically an indication of the heat being transmitted by a body. An infrared detector typically consists of a phototransistor or photodiode, whereby the electrical characteristics of the device are directly affected by the intensity of the infrared signal being measured. They are generally relatively low-cost and fairly robust.

Because the device is measuring infrared signals it is particularly useful at night, and hence has direct military applications. Indeed, in bright sunlight or under high internal lighting such sensors do not operate particularly well. For robot AI uses they are therefore very useful as an additional sensor to detect the heat of a body. They can also be used in a similar way to sonar sensors, by bouncing an infrared signal off an object to detect the presence of (and distance to) the object. However, within a laboratory environment, light intensity can cause considerable problems, even to the extent of making the sensor almost useless.

AUDIO DETECTION

We have previously discussed the possibility of an AI system communicating with a human to the extent that the human cannot distinguish between the system and a human – this was the basis of the Turing Test discussion in Chapter 3. But that was based on the concept of keyboard entry and screen output. It is also quite possible for a computer system to detect and respond to different sounds.

The more pronounced the sound, the easier the problem becomes to resolve. To this extent, onset detection can be used merely when a signal rises sharply in amplitude to an initial peak. A hand clap or loud bang is a good example of a signal that can readily be detected. However, more of interest in terms of robot interaction is **voice activity detection** (VAD).

With VAD, specific values or features of the audio signal are used to cause a robot or computer system to operate in different ways. Once the audio features have been obtained, the result can be classified as to the nature of the signal that has been witnessed, particularly if it has overcome previously specified threshold levels which characterise the signal type.

VAD IN NOISE

Often with audio input, considerable noise is present (e.g. background noise). This means that a compromise needs to be drawn between a human voice being detected as noise and/or noise being detected as a voice. In such circumstances it is often desirable that VAD should be fail-safe, indicating speech has been detected even when the decision is in doubt, thereby lowering the chances of losing speech segments.

One problem for VAD under heavy noise conditions is the percentage of pauses during speech and the reliability in the detection of these intervals and when speech starts up again. Although it can be useful to have a low percentage of speech activity, clipping, which is the loss of the start of active speech, should be minimised to preserve quality.

TELEMARKETING AI

One interesting application of VAD in AI systems is the employment of predictive diallers, used extensively by telemarketing firms. To maximise (human) agent productivity, such firms use predictive diallers to call more numbers than they have agents available, knowing most calls will end up in either ringing out with no answer or an answering machine will come on line.

When a person answers, they typically speak very briefly, merely saying 'Hello' perhaps, and then there is a short period of silence. Answering machine messages, on the other hand, usually contain 10–15 seconds of continuous speech. It is not difficult to set VAD parameters to determine whether a person or a machine answered the call, and if it is a person, transfer the call to an available agent. The important thing is for the system to operate 'correctly' in the vast majority of cases – it doesn't have to be perfect.

If the system detects what it believes to be an answering machine, the system hangs up. Sometimes the system correctly detects a person answering the call, but no agent is available, leaving the person shouting 'Hello, Hello' into the phone, wondering why no one is on the other end. Due to its cost-effectiveness it is anticipated that AI will be used far more extensively in this field in the years ahead – particularly in terms of detecting (potential purchasing) characteristics of the person answering the telephone based on the first words they utter.

SMELL

An automated sense of smell is referred to as **machine olfaction**. As with classical AI techniques, in practice it is based mainly on attempting to copy, in some way, the human sense of smell, even though this is a very individual, subjective entity. The underlying technology is still in the relatively early stages of development, but the wide range of potential application areas indicates that a commercial drive may not be far away. There are application opportunities with drug and explosives detection, for example, as well as uses in food processing, perfumery and chemical compound monitoring.

The main implement is the electronic nose. This consists of an array of sensors with associated electronics to convert scents to digital signals and for data processing such as in a computer. The overall nose system is then expected to convert the sensor responses into an odour output. A nose is 'trained' by subjecting it to a target odour; it is then required to 'recognise' future smells as being either alike or not to the original.

Electronic noses are also useful for olfactive nuisance monitoring of the environment, particularly surveying notorious sewerage systems in an attempt to keep them in check. However, for the most part such sensor systems are rather large and in many cases not very readily portable. They are also rather slow in carrying out an analysis and may take some time before they are ready for a second or further analysis. As such, their role in AI systems is somewhat limited at present.

TASTE

Just as there are electronic noses for smell, so there are electronic tongues (e-tongues) for taste. Again, it is more a question of copying human taste. Sensors detect the same organic or inorganic compounds perceived by human taste receptors. For a particular taste, information from the separate sensors is fused together to fit a unique identifying pattern. In this case it is apparent that the detection abilities of an e-tongue are far more sensitive (i.e. much better) than those of its human counterpart.

The sensory results from an e-tongue are dealt with in a similar way to the human case. Electronic signals produced are perceived in terms of pattern recognition – attempting to match a new set of sensor readings with a database of memorised taste spectra. Due to the nature of the sensors, liquid samples can usually be analysed directly, whereas solids require dissolving before they can be dealt with. The difference between each sensor's actual reading and the value of a reference electrode is obtained and used for calculations.

E-tongues (which don't tend to look anything like biological tongues!) have numerous application areas, particularly, as one might expect, in the food and drink industry. These include the assessment of flavourings, as well as analysing drinks of both the alcoholic and non-alcoholic variety for quality purposes. The range of uses also includes sweet syrups, various powders and dissolvable tablets. Salt and caffeine detectors are relatively easy and cheap to operate when required.

It is the case, however, that e-tongues are not normally designed to be carried around on a small mobile robot. The sense of taste is quite specific to human nutrition and hence it only has a limited role to play in AI systems – indeed, no real role at all in A-life! Its main function is as a technical assistance to human taste testing due to its standardising properties and reliability.

ULTRAVIOLET DETECTION

Ultraviolet light is a form of electro-magnetic radiation. It has a shorter wavelength than visible light but longer wavelength than X-rays. It is referred to as ultraviolet as it is made up of electro-magnetic waves with frequencies higher than those identified with the colour violet. It is not something that is apparently directly sensed and acted upon by humans. It is found in abundance in sunlight and appears in electric arcs and other phenomena.

Ultraviolet light can be detected by photodiodes relatively easily; indeed, a variety of relatively low-cost detection devices is available. For the most part they are fairly small and certainly portable. Often they are based on an extension of sensors used to detect visible light – as a result they can sometimes be troubled by an undesirable response to visible light and inherent instabilities.

Ultraviolet sensors can potentially be employed for AI systems. They are, in this case, particularly useful if a robot's energy supply contains solar cells that need recharging from sunlight – hence making them useful for real A-life robots, as the sensor can be used, for example, to indicate the direction the robot needs to face in order to charge its energy supplies.

X-RAY

X-rays have a shorter wavelength than ultraviolet rays, but a longer wavelength than gamma rays. They are generally regarded as invisible to the human eye, although extreme experiments have indicated that there may be some slight recognition in certain circumstances. In medical applications X-rays are produced by firing electrons at a metal target – the resultant X-rays are absorbed by human bones but not so much by tissue, so a sensitive photographic plate can be employed to obtain a two-dimensional visual image of the result from firing X-rays at parts of a human body.

There is a wide range of X-ray sensors available, such as semiconductor array detectors. These are mainly small, portable and generally accurate and reliable. They can therefore be employed for AI systems, should the application need arise!

CONCLUDING REMARKS

It is a big advantage of AI in comparison with human intelligence that the potential range of sensory input is extremely broad, whereas human senses are limited. On top of this limitation, the frequency range of signals sensed by humans is very small – the visible light spectrum (humans' main sensory input) is nowhere near as broad as the infrared spectrum alone.

AI can potentially sense signals not directly available to humans (other than by means of a conversion to a human sense, such as X-ray converted to a two-dimensional visual image). As we have seen, X-rays and ultraviolet light can be used as sensory input by a machine, but so too can sensed gamma radiation, microwaves, water vapour detection and so on – all that was done in this chapter was to give a brief overview of some of the most obvious.

One issue, however, as we saw with classical AI, in terms of intelligence in general, is the limited capabilities of human thought in conceiving of non-human applications such as those that might be useful for a robot. Therefore, most present-day applications of non-human sensors are to convert signals into energy that humans can sense, such as an X-ray visual image. The employment of the potential wide range of sensory input by AI systems in their own right will clearly increase their range of abilities as time passes.

KEY TERMS

atomic segments, correspondence problem, ensemble averaging, grey level, growing (segments), local averaging, machine olfaction, model matching, passive triangulation, pattern matching, picture matrix, pixel differentiation, point tracking, radio frequency identification device, reed switches, splitting (segments), strain gauge, triangulation, voice activity detection

FURTHER READING

1   *Computer Vision: Algorithms and Applications* by R. Szeliski, published by Springer, 2010. This title discusses the current state-of-the-art in computer vision, looking at the problems encountered and the types of algorithms employed. It is certainly a good, modern next step in the field.

2   *Making Robots Smarter: Combining Sensing and Action through Robot Learning* by K. Morik, M. Kaiser and V. Klingspor, published by Springer, 1999. This is good as a general follow-on from this chapter or the previous one. It considers learning in robots as a part of a sensor/action feedback loop.

3   *Autonomous Mobile Robots: Sensing, Control, Decision Making and Applications* by S.S. Ge, published by CRC Press, 2006. This is a comprehensive reference looking at the theoretical, technical and practical aspects of the field. It examines in detail the key components involved, including sensors and sensor fusion.

4   *Robotic Tactile Sensing: Technologies and System* by R. Dahiya and M. Valle, published by Springer, 2011. An in-depth look at robot touch, including such issues as shape, texture, hardness and material type. It offers comprehensive coverage, including rolling between fingers and sensing arrays.

GLOSSARY

artificial life the recreation of biological life by technological means.

artificial neural network an interconnected group of artificial neurons (brain cells) using computational, mathematical or technological models.

atomic segments used in image segment growing; initially small groups of pixels with very similar greyscale values are identified.

average interrogator Alan Turing's name for a typical individual involved as a judge in his imitation game, trying to differentiate a machine from a human.

best first search exploring a problem by expanding the best (most promising) option in the next level.

brain-in-a-vat experiment a philosophical argument involving a disembodied brain, kept alive, yet fully experiencing life.

bucket brigade a system used to pass on rewards from one rule to another.

cellular automata a regular grid of cells in which each one has finite states that can be affected by neighbouring cells.

collective intelligence shared or group intelligence arising from cooperation between individuals.

common sense knowledge the collection of facts and information that an ordinary person would know.

consciousness subjective experience, awareness and executive control of the mind.

embodiment giving a brain (or artificial neural network) a body in order for it to interact with the real world.

ensemble averaging the average value of the same pixel taken over several time steps.

epiphenomenal mental states can be caused by physical effects but cause no resultant physical output themselves.

fitness function used to calculate the overall value of a member of the population in a genetic algorithm in terms of its different characteristics.

frames an AI structure used to divide knowledge into substructures.

free will the ability to make choices, free from constraints.

fuzzy trees method of splitting a database into different regions, where the same piece of information can appear (to some extent) in several branches.

Garden of Eden patterns in cellular automata, particular patterns which cannot be realised from any previous pattern.

goal-based agent an autonomous entity which observes and acts upon an environment and directs its activity towards achieving goals.

greedy best first search use of a heuristic to predict how close the end of a path is to a solution; paths which are closer to a solution are extended first.

grey level representation of an image pixel between black and white.

growing (segments) the method used to grow regions in an image from atomic segments by associating areas with similar pixel values.

hill climbing an iterative procedure that attempts to find a better solution to a problem by making small changes. If a change produces a better solution, the new solution is retained, repeating until no further improvements can be found.

learning agent an agent which can operate in unknown environments and improve through learning, using feedback to determine how its performance should be modified.

linearly separable problem when represented as a pattern space, it requires only one straight cut to separate all of the patterns of one type in the space from all of the patterns of another type.

local averaging the value of a pixel is replaced with the average value of local pixels.

local search   moving from solution to solution amongst candidate problem solutions until an optimal solution is found.

machine olfaction   sense of smell in a machine.

model matching   matching edge candidates in an image with an edge model.

model-based agent   an agent which can handle a partially observable environment. Its current state is stored, describing the part of the world which cannot be seen. This knowledge is called a model of the world.

multiagents   use of several agents in a cooperative fashion, each providing a partial answer to a problem.

new media   media which emerged in the latter part of the twentieth century. On-demand access to (digitised) content any time, any where, on any digital device, with user feedback and creative participation.

passive triangulation   distance measurement to an object using a two-camera system; it requires the position of a corresponding point in the two images to be known, along with the distance between the cameras.

pattern matching   in image processing, comparing a number of edge candidates with a previously defined edge pattern.

perceptron   a binary classifier as the simplest form of neuron model.

picture matrix   an array of image pixel values representing the scene viewed.

pixel differentiation   the rate of change/difference of values between picture elements.

point tracking   tracing an image object outline by joining the points that have been selected as edge candidates.

radio frequency identification device   technology using radio communication to exchange data between a tag and a reader (computer) for the purpose of identification.

reed switches   electrical switches operated by applying a magnetic field.

reflex agent   an agent in which historical data is ignored.

splitting (segments)   the method used to divide an image into regions by breaking up the image into areas with similar pixel values.

steepest descent to find a local minimum of a function using steepest (or gradient) descent, steps taken are proportional to the gradient of the function at a point.

strain gauge a device used to measure the strain of an object, usually due to a change of electrical resistance as the material changes in length.

strong AI machines can think in the same way as humans.

subsumption architecture intelligent behaviour is decomposed into several simple behavioural layers; each layer has its own goal; higher layers are more abstract.

symbolic processing creating AI using high-level symbols, as in conventional computer programming.

temporal difference algorithm a method of learning in which the difference between the estimated reward and the actual reward received is paired with a stimulus that also reflects a future reward.

three laws of robotics a set of three rules written by author Isaac Asimov by which robots are programmed to behave with regard to humans.

triangulation determining the distance to a point by measuring angles to it from known points.

voice activity detection technique in which the presence or absence of human speech can be detected.

weak AI machines can demonstrate intelligence but are not necessarily conscious like a human mind.

INDEX

action potentials 90
active triangulation 162
actuators 16
adoptee intelligence 26
alien view 18, 68
A-life 117–18
AND operator 41, 95, 133
animal intelligence 14
ant colony optimisation 137
ant studies 123
agents 7, 108
argument from disability 84
Aristotle 24
artificial life 116–17
artificial neural network (ANN)
    92–101, 108, 125
Asimov 75
atomic segments 159
audio detection 169
autonomous agents 109
average interrogator 78
axons 90

backward chaining 36
Beckham 27
bees 14, 63
behavioural models 119
best first search 49
bidirectional search 46
binary chromosome 103, 105–6
Binet 14, 21
biological AI 139

biological brain 10, 11, 89, 139
biological definition/life 18
biological inspiration 137
Blue brain 7
blocks world 160
bottom-up approach 88
brain size 15
bucket brigade technique 53
brain-in-a-vat experiment 65
brain prosthesis experiment 69
breadth-first search 45
Burt 26

CCD camera 147
cell body 90
cellular automata 119
centre of gravity method 42
cerebral cortex 97
chatterbots 4
chess 48
chimpanzees 15, 63
Chinese room 5, 28, 72–4, 85
classical AI 1, 31–59, 88
classifications 95
co-evolution 128
collective intelligence 134
colour 149, 159
combinatorial explosion 38
common sense knowledge 50
common sense reasoning 5
comparative intelligence 27
complex behaviour 122

computer chromosomes 102
conductive rubber 167
conflict resolution 33
connectivity 15
consciousness 65, 67, 70, 73, 78, 86, 142, 143
convex/concave features 161
correlations 55
correspondence problem 162
creativity 80
crossover operator 104
culturing neurons 139
cyborgs 11
cybernetics 11
cyclops fish 125–6

DARPA grand challenge 7
Darwin 25
data mining 54; applications 58
decision trees 56
Deep Blue 7, 48
definition of intelligence 13, 17, 116
defuzzification 42–3
demons 51
dendrites 90
depth-first search 45
depth-limited search 46
Descartes 2
discriminator 101
DNA 55
dolphins 20

Edmonds 3
edge detection 152
ego (agent) 111
Einstein 27
Elbot 81, 83
electrical interface 140
electrode array 140, 141
electronic nose 171
electronic tongue 171
ELIZA 4
embodiment 10, 140
emergence (of consciousness) 73, 74, 143
emergent behaviour 108

energy usage 16
energy value 134
ensemble averaging 151
epiphenomenal 70, 73
evolutionary computing 102
evolving A-life 125
excitatory signals 90
expert systems 6, 32; fuzzy 43; problems with 37

financial systems 7
finite state machines 119
firing rules 35
fitness function 104, 107
force sensing 168
forward chaining 35
frames 50
free will 66
fuzzification 39, 43
fuzzy logic 39
fuzzy rules 40
fuzzy sets 3
fuzzy trees 57

Galatea 2
Galton 21
game of life 120
Garden of Eden patterns 124
gene pool 128
general problem solver 3
genetic algorithms 8, 102–7; examples 105, 126
gliders 121
global solution 49, 107
goal-based agents 111
Golem 2, 128
greedy best first search 49
grey level 149

habitual learning 141
HAL 9000 9
hardware agents 112
hardware robots 129
Hawking 76
herons 15
heuristic searching 49

hidden humans 78
highest priority rule 34
hill climbing 49
human-centric 29, 74
Human Genome Project 54
human intelligence 9
human language 4, 74, 86
humanness 82
human neurons 11, 142
hybrid systems 138

IF/THEN statements 33, 40, 52
image analysis 149
image pixels 148
image spectrum 152
image transformation 148
image understanding 160
infrared detectors 168
inhibitory signals 90
intelligence 13, 63, 116
intelligent water drops 138
IQ tests 20

Jabberwacky 80–1
Jerome 48
jokes 80
judges 80

Kasparov 7, 48
knowledge-based systems 32
knowledge representation 49
Kurzweil 10, 75

lasers 163
learning 39, 94
learning agents 111
Le Bon 15
life 117
linearly separable problem 95
line finding 155
local averaging 150
local search 49
local minimum 49
Loebner 79, 81
Loehlin 26
lower competence action 113

machine learning 52
magnetic sensors 164
map building 113
March of the Machines 10
mating 102, 126
Matrix, The 66
maze solving 48
McCarthy 3, 5, 6
McCulloch and Pitts 2, 6, 93
memory 18
methods and demons 51
mexican hat 98
micro switch 165
Mill, John Stuart 25
mind children 75
Minneapolis (twin studies) 26
Minsky 3–5, 9, 31, 64
model-based agents 111
model matching 156
modern AI 88
Moore's law 7, 10
Moravec 75
motor neurons 90
movement 17, 161
multiagents 111
multiple rules 34
mutation 103
MYCIN 32

natural language 5, 110
nature-versus-nurture 23
nerve cell 89
neural networks 8
neuron model 92
neurons 70, 89, 99, 139
new media 135
noise 150
N-tuple network 98–101

octopus 14
On the Origin of Species 25
optical sensors 168
OR operator 41

Papert 4
particle swarm optimization 137

passive triangulation 162
pattern matching 156
Penrose 62–4, 71, 142
perceptrons 4, 94
performance probability 130
philosophy (of AI) 60–87
picture matrix 149
pixel differentiation 153
plastic brain 91
Plato 24
point tracking 156
population evolution 123
population of solutions 102
population size 103, 107
predator–prey co-evolution 127
priority grading 111
problem solving 44, 108
proximity sensors 165

Quillan 5

radar 164
Random Access Memory (RAM) 99
random behaviours 62
randomness (brain) 62
Rational AI 68
real-life inspiration 122
real-life modification 122
reed switches 164
reflex agent 110
reinforcement learning 39, 131;
    problems 132
reversible cellular automata 124
RFID 166
Rickman 80
Roberts 81
Roberts cross operator 153
robot mouse 132
robotics 6, 106, 112
robots 110–44
Rubik's cube 48
rule-based systems 32, 52
rule prioritization 43

searches 45, 46
search examples 47, 48

searching problems 47
Searle 5, 72, 142
segment analysis 158
segment growing 158, 159
segment splitting 158
self awareness 67
self-organizing network 96
sense of humour 84
sensing 16, 146–74
seven dwarf robots 129
Shannon 3
shared intelligence 135
sharks 20
Simon 32
simulated A-Life 118
simulated evolution 126
simulation 62
singularity 74
slots 50
slugs and snails 90
smell 171
social bias 19
software agents 109
spiders 14
steepest descent 49
stereo vision 146
stochastic diffusion search 138
stock market predictions 135
strain gauge 168
strong AI 65
sub-frames 50
subjective intelligence 18, 23, 28, 64
subservience 63
subsumption architecture 109, 112
supermarket shopping
swarm intelligence 136
symbolic processing 68
synapses 90

taste 171
technological singularity 74
telemarketing 170
telephone exchange 63
template matching 155
temporal difference algorithms 133
three laws of robotics 75

Three Men in a Boat 48
threshold value 90, 94, 154, 157
totalistic cellular automata 123
touch 167
triangulation 162
Turing 2, 5, 76, 79, 83, 86
Turing test 72, 76–85
twins 26

Ultra Hal 82
ultrasound 17, 130, 163
ultraviolet 17, 172
understanding 13, 49, 63, 72, 74, 84

validity (IQ tests) 22
vehicle guidance 44
Vinge 75
virtual worlds 10, 125, 128
vision 146
visual cortex 150

vitamin C 22
voice activity detection 169

water spiders 14
weak AI 64
weighted average method 42
weightings (neurons) 93
weightless network 98
Wells 135
when-changed method 51
when-needed method 51
Wikipedia 135
wireless technology 8
world brain 135
wrap-around 121

X-ray 17, 173

Zadeh 3